LEADERSHIP KHICHDI

Made Simple

ACTIONS THAT CREATE LONG-LASTING IMPACTS
VOLUME 1 – THE SME & STARTUP VERSION

DR. YOGESH PAWAR

First Edition: February 2023
Copyright © Dr. Yogesh Pawar 2023
All Rights Reserved.

ISBN 979-8-88909-883-6

Author Contact:
Dr. Yogesh Pawar,
School of Inspirational Leadership Pvt. Ltd.,
Office No. 205A, Regent Plaza,
Baner-Pashan Link Rd.,
Baner, Pune - 411045.
Contact: +91 91686 87711
Landline: 020 2991 0979
yogesh@sileadership.com
www.siluniversity.com

DEDICATION

This book is dedicated to

The amazing founders of various Micro, Small, and Medium Enterprises, and startups that go a long way in providing solutions to make life easy and also play a definitive role in nation-building.

My amazing family who let me explore this huge ocean of Entrepreneurship and helped me establish the School of Inspirational Leadership as a trusted and respected consulting company in our country.

My grandmother who, without any education or experience, created a fortune for all of us. The seed of entrepreneurship was sown in me by her and she remains my guiding light even today.

ADVANCE PRAISE FOR THE BOOK

1. Finally, a book that will handhold you, the enterprising entrepreneur, to understand and build winning leadership skills. Dr. Yogesh Pawar, a qualified mentor, who has helped numerous SME and MSME entrepreneurs to scale up their businesses, has effectively explained the thought behind each leadership principle, accompanied by effective tools. This book has the immense power to change the future of your business.

   Chetan Dharia, Managing Director, Anant Defence Systems Pvt. Ltd.

2. As an entrepreneur, I have experienced the challenges of leadership time and again. I am glad to know that there is a book that will help young and upcoming entrepreneurs to understand and deal with such challenges by using the right tools and techniques in the right way.

   Mohan Anturkar, Founder, M Square Engineers

3. There is a lot of entrepreneurship energy in India. People have the aspirations, enthusiasm and ideas to start something new, to be successful, and are willing to take risks and embrace discomfort. However, in order to succeed as an entrepreneur, having an innovative idea is not enough. To be successful, entrepreneurs need sound leadership skills to be able to navigate the external VUCA world as well as to ensure that they take the entire organization with them. *Leadership Khichdi Made Simple* is a book specially written keeping in mind the needs of SME and startup entrepreneurs. Yogesh is the best person to

write this book, having trained, consulted, and mentored 700+ enterprises. He uses lucid language and real-life examples to impart the tried and tested wisdom from his experiences. A must-read for all entrepreneurs.

Major General Neeraj Bali (Retd.), Specialist – Culture and Organizational Behavior, School of Inspirational Leadership

4. Are leaders born or can they be made? My experience is that although each one of us has leadership skills inherent in us, a good mentor like Dr. Yogesh Pawar can indeed hone and polish these skills and also teach us new skills that are useful to build, sustain and scale up our enterprises in the dynamic world of today. The book *Leadership Khichdi Made Simple* is an attempt to present the nutritious knowledge of leadership in small, and easily digestible bits for better understanding and implementation. I would encourage entrepreneurs, founders, and leaders at all levels in any organization to read and learn from the book.

   Amit Arokar, Founder and Managing Director, ECE India Energies Pvt. Ltd.

5. Kudos to Dr. Yogesh Pawar for rightly identifying the need for such a book for entrepreneurs, startup founders, and leaders at all levels in any organization. Right from understanding how great leaders create personal rituals to creating impactful organizations, making the journey enjoyable, understanding what great leaders don't do, and the habits of great leaders, *Leadership Khichdi Made Simple* covers it all. It addresses the various challenges faced by leaders in the current volatile business scenario and gives them new insights into leading their talent and organization to success.

   Gautam Malhotra, Director, Gardens Need

THIS BOOK IS FOR

- Entrepreneurs and founders of SMEs and startups, interested in scaling up, restructuring, or sustaining their businesses
- Anyone who wishes to understand how good leadership can be a game-changer for business

The book is also highly useful for aspiring leaders and managers in the corporate sector.

How to get the most out of this book?

1. There are two important desires that can help you get the most out of this book.

   a. Your desire to understand humans and their various facets through which, you can explore your leadership.
   b. Your desire to create an organization that can scale up through people.

2. As a leader, you can develop these desires by constantly reminding yourself about the bigger picture that you visualize for yourself and your organization. Developing these desires will help you paint a picture of your future for a more fulfilling professional, social and personal life. Say to yourself repeatedly, "My goal is to create an organization and grow it, and this knowledge lies in this book. If I am conscious about these elements, I will be able to scale up any business that I undertake." Certain change principles narrated in this book are applicable to entrepreneurs only. However, most of

them are applicable and beneficial to leaders, managers, and entrepreneurs.

3. Read each chapter twice – the first time, to understand the overall objectives of Leadership, and to reflect on whether the contents of the book are relevant to you and your environment. Jot down what comes to mind as you go through it. You will probably be tempted to move forward after doing this. However, I would request you to read the chapter a second time so that you fully understand every aspect it covers.

4. Write down *your own* interpretation of each chapter. (Utilize the space given after each chapter for this purpose). You can use your notes for future reference. Ask yourself, "What/Why/Where/How can I implement these concepts in my environment, and if I can't, why not?

5. Implement the understanding derived from each chapter in all your surrounding environments: personal, professional, and social. Observe the effects, mostly positive, and then move on to implement the understanding derived from the next chapter.

This book has the capability to change three things in you.

i. It will start affecting you positively at the individual level.
ii. It will start changing how you operate at your workplace (marketplace) positively.
iii. It will change your financials positively.

CONTENTS

FOREWORD

The word, "Khichdi," in the title of Yogesh's book on leadership, caught my eye. The word sounded like the name of a cool science fiction movie. Later, I came to know of its meaning as a ubiquitous, nutritious, and well-liked dish across India. Colloquially, it was also used to refer to a mixture of a few things that needed to be sorted out in order to turn something into a success.

The words "Leadership" and "Khichdi" coming together make sense if you think about sorting out the leadership mixture to create a recipe for organizational success. What a GREAT title, I thought – "Leadership Khichdi Made Simple"!

As the title suggests, the connection to Leadership is obvious. Good Leadership is indeed a mixture of skills, attributes, positive attitudes, behaviors, and actions that one needs to understand, sort out and inculcate in the right quantities, in the right way. When leaders get it right, their leadership is indeed nourishing and can change the destiny of organizations, the people who work with them, and in turn, the people they serve.

But how does a leader get it right continuously, considering the pandemic-enhanced VUCA world that businesses operate in? I have known Yogesh since he became certified in Directive Communication Psychology back in 2009, and have followed his success with consulting and coaching throughout the years... his experience is diverse enough to Get it Right! And it is so appropriate that he is sharing his experience in this book.

Starting from the very basics of **Understanding How Great Leaders Create Personal and Organizational Rituals,** in the first chapter, Yogesh has gone beyond the tried and tested Conscious Competence Model by Noel Burch, to develop the **Beyond Conscious Competence Model** through his experience and observations. Each chapter delivers knowledge in lucid, bite-sized pieces and also gets the reader to work with the chapter and introspect before applying all that he has learned.

Also of special importance is the sixth chapter, which talks about **What Successful Leaders Don't Do** – a topic less addressed while talking about Leadership. Yogesh ends his book with his masterstroke by introducing the **Habits of Great Leaders** and the concept of **PEARL in the Heart of Great Leaders – Proactivity, Engagement, Appreciation, Recognition, and Listening.** By encouraging leaders to evaluate themselves on these parameters, Yogesh goes further to engage the readers by inviting them to take up the 21-day challenge for PEARL implementation.

With the number of startups only growing and business environments undergoing dramatic change, not *good* but *great* leadership is a necessity that businesses cannot do without. *Leadership Khichdi Made Simple* is ideally poised to make a positive difference to the leadership of the entrepreneur, the founder, and the aspirational manager to create successful and meaningful businesses, with happy and engaged teams, serving delighted consumers.

– **Arthur F. Carmazzi**
Founder of Directive Communication Inc.

PREFACE

Here's something to think about! We are a densely populated planet with billions of people and the numbers are only growing! If so, why do we still have people constraints in almost every organization?

The availability of manpower can be compared to the availability of seawater. In the case of seawater, the challenge is how much of it can be used for drinking. Just as seawater needs to undergo treatment to become potable, similarly, people resources need to undergo a transformation in order to perform as per new-age demands. These resources are an ever-growing challenge for every organization because "People" are the only resources in an organization that can think and feel. The rest can all be automated and standardized. Organizations and leaders who understand this, create a unique methodology that is relevant to their organization and produce innovation, change, and a bright future in the marketplace.

But the key questions are –

1. What kind of people should companies hire, retain, and train?
2. What kind of leadership is required in a world that is so interconnected but still individualistic?
3. How do leaders create a personal brand that leads to nurturing and creating high-performing talent in the organization?
4. How do organizations produce leaders that create a legacy in the marketplace?
5. How does a leader form the right balance between the emotions of people and the economics of the business?

Libraries and the Internet are full of books on management and the various skills required for leaders to lead, and every piece of literature is the right opinion of the author. But is there a book that speaks about the relevant patterns and actions that leaders need to take in the new era of leadership?

Yes, there is now such a book – *Leadership Khichdi Made Simple*! It stands out because of its very different perspective, approach, and lucid language, keeping the basic principles of man-management intact.

"Khichdi" is a Hindi word and does not exist in the English language, but the literal translation of the word means, "a soothing mixture of lentils, spices, and rice in the form of a recipe that is delicious and tasty." It is a word that the common Indian immediately relates to, a dish that is prepared in almost every household in India and cherished by all family members. Likewise, leadership too is made up of many elements, attributes, attitudes, skills, behaviors, and actions. If all these elements are acquired and used by a leader in the right quantity, in the right recipe, it can change the face of any organization and take it to greater heights. The challenge here is that leaders, entrepreneurs, and managers either form a bias about all these elements or stick to old beliefs about how they should lead, and hence miss out on results in the marketplace.

In the last 50 years, we have seen new legacy businesses being created globally. Structured businesses have been struggling for leadership talent, while beginners fail to attract them. So the question is – where is this leadership talent – should it be created or should one look for it? What is the secret behind the sound leadership culture of an organization?

This book uncovers the answers to the above questions in a unique way such that they can be implemented by every leader across the globe. It gives you a new way of leading your talent. I define this as "Legacy Leadership."

This book has other distinctive ideas on how to use the tools and methods that will assist entrepreneurs, founders, leaders, and aspirational managers globally to take a deep dive and reform their old beliefs about leading people and their organizations.

As I always say, "The same information repeated over a period of time in various forms creates a belief system." To do this, the organization's founders, leaders, and aspirational managers should have a clear and scientifically crafted vision of the future. This book also specifically mentions "What leaders shouldn't do," which is a novel way of identifying the red flags in the life and behavior of leaders, and how these can be avoided or overcome.

Leaders who want to scale up their businesses or roles are not only operating in complex business and resource-constrained markets but also have to deal with the ever-changing dynamics that lead to volatility and uncertainty in the marketplace. Hence, those among them who are able to anticipate change and take relevant risks will score high and achieve greater heights if they create a cause that is worth it.

That's how this book is relevant to new-age entrepreneurs, founders, leaders, and aspirational managers globally.

– Yogesh Pawar

Acknowledgements

I take this opportunity to express my gratitude to all my teachers who selflessly taught me and came to me in various forms, from various walks of life, in various instances, and made me who I am today. In particular, I would like to mention Arthur F. Carmazzi, from whom I learned how the psychology of communication can be taught in a fun way.

I profusely thank all the leaders who gave me experiences that enriched me and the thousands of entrepreneurs who gave me opportunities to work with them while managing the change processes in their organizations.

I appreciate the huge efforts of all my business associates and employees at the School of Inspirational Leadership, and their sincerity and dedication to its vision, mission, and goals.

My sincere thanks to the editorial and publishing team of Notion Press for their timely input, and for giving the book the shape that it is in today. And a special mention of the one who worked with me very closely while giving shape to *Leadership Khichdi Made Simple*, Yogita Vaidya.

Last but not the least, I wish to express my eternal gratitude and love to my greatest strength – my family.

CHAPTER 1

Understanding How Great Leaders Create Personal and Organizational Rituals

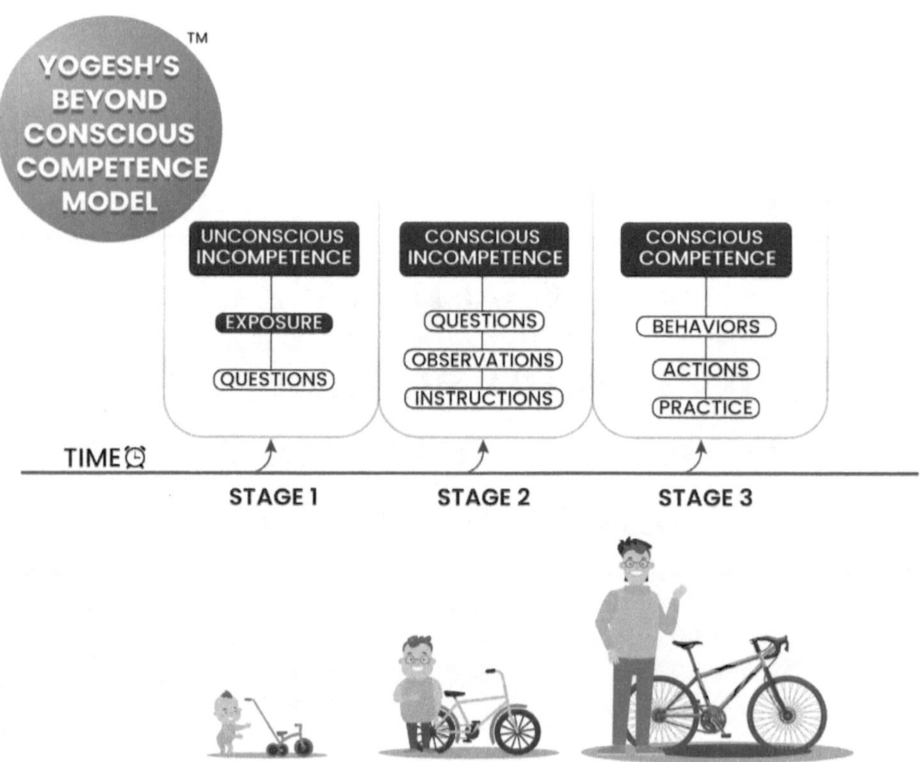

Fig. 1 Yogesh's Beyond Conscious Competence Model

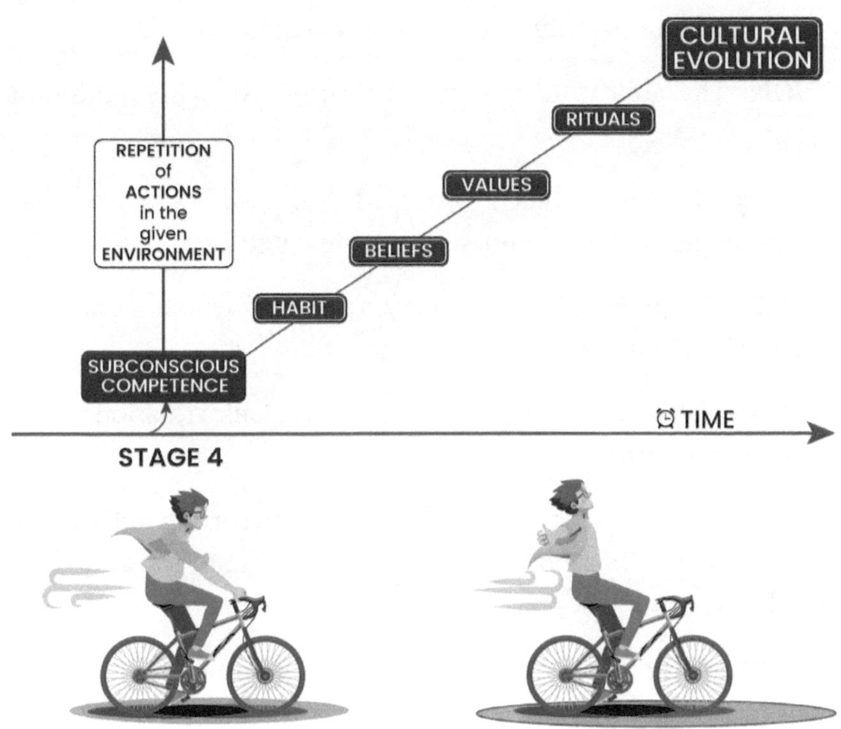
CULTURAL
EVOLUTION
RITUALS
VALUES
BELIEFS
HABIT
REPETITION
of
ACTIONS
in the
given
ENVIRONMENT
SUBCONSCIOUS
COMPETENCE
TIME
STAGE 4

Understanding the Terminology

COMPETENCE: The ability to execute certain tasks with the correct (according to the desired environment) behaviors.

INCOMPETENCE: The inability to execute certain tasks with the correct (according to the desired environment) behaviors.

CONSCIOUS: The awareness of the as-is situation(s).

SUBCONSCIOUS: The unawareness of the as-is situation(s) or action taken with minimum effort due to its being repeated over time.

REPETITION: The ability to conduct the same task with minimum variation.

HABIT: The ability to conduct a task with less awareness, and that which causes disturbances to humans when deviated from.

ENVIRONMENT: A geographical territory, a group of people, situations, or processes specifically created, or an ecosystem.

BELIEFS: Assumptions experienced through various situations over the duration of a lifetime.

VALUES: Guiding principles that are personalized to certain individuals or groups of people/institutions, which guide them toward their statement of purpose, cause, or calling.

CULTURE: People accepting each other with common beliefs and values.

RITUALS: Behaviors/actions which are not questioned, and which, when challenged, may cause disturbances in society.

These are the parameters of creating a sustainable, scalable organization and in the process also ensuring that the happiness quotient of everyone involved is high.

NOTE: Throughout the book, there are relevant examples of how leaders across the globe have implemented the Beyond Conscious Competence Model. These examples will help you derive a Beyond Conscious Competence Model that is relevant to your situation and help you implement scalable processes for the same.

The journey of a leader's performance in the marketplace always begins with emotions and ends with economics. Hence, it is recommended that all the parameters given in the Beyond Conscious Competence Model are carefully observed by the leader. The leader must drive the organization based on a *value system*, which acts as *a foundation force* for building up a scalable organization that positively impacts the world. The method of creating such an organization is different for different organizations. However, the foundation of values creates a common understanding among the stakeholders about why the organization exists.

> *The journey of a leader's performance in the marketplace always begins with emotions and ends with economics.*
>
> *— Yogesh Pawar*

Creating a Value System

A Value System is a set of timeless guiding principles specifically created for an organization, requiring no external justification.

If you are a leader or a manager of an organization, you will be able to perform extraordinarily well if you are in sync with the organization's value system, or if you work towards your organization's value system. Create systems, processes, rituals, and behaviors in the organization that support its value system. *Rituals are behaviors/actions that are to be repeated in order to reinforce the values of the organization.* As a leader, it is you who will define which daily actions need to be converted into organization rituals. Or, which rituals should be converted into the belief system or value system in your organization.

However, as a manager, you may have limitations while doing the above and may have to adopt the existing organizational rituals. But as an entrepreneur, you have the scope to create your own organization's beliefs, values, or rituals. For leaders, it is a must that you join an organization that has a value system similar to your own. It helps you to acclimatize to the organization quickly and perform better. It also gives you more satisfaction to perform in an organization that has the same values as you – your decision-making is smooth and it gathers speed for continuous improvement.

As a leader, you should identify your value system and align it with your organization's value system. You will then be able to step up the corporate ladder and will find yourself in a better position in the organization. In order to identify your value system, I recommend the Value Card Method, which is mentioned further in this chapter. You can identify the values that originally exist in the organization in various ways: by studying how the organization has grown in the past, how it comes up with new products and services, and how stable it is in the market. Employees, former and current, can also give you information about the culture of the organization, which will help you understand the beliefs of the organization and its value system.

If you are an entrepreneur, you will have the power to choose how you want to create your company. You must first identify your value system by using the Value Card Method and ensure that you create the vision, strategies, procedures, guidelines, and performance indicators of the organization based on your value system. Now, you need to repeatedly imbibe these values into everyone in the organization, in various forms.

> *The foundation pillar of values creates a common understanding among the stakeholders about how the organization needs to function.*
>
> *– Yogesh Pawar*

Organization Maturity Cycle

Whether you are a leader or an entrepreneur, how you drive the value system in the organization, will depend on the Organization Maturity Cycle.

Every organization needs to go through an Organization Maturity Cycle. This cycle is depicted in the following three phases: Struggle, Stability, and Scalability.

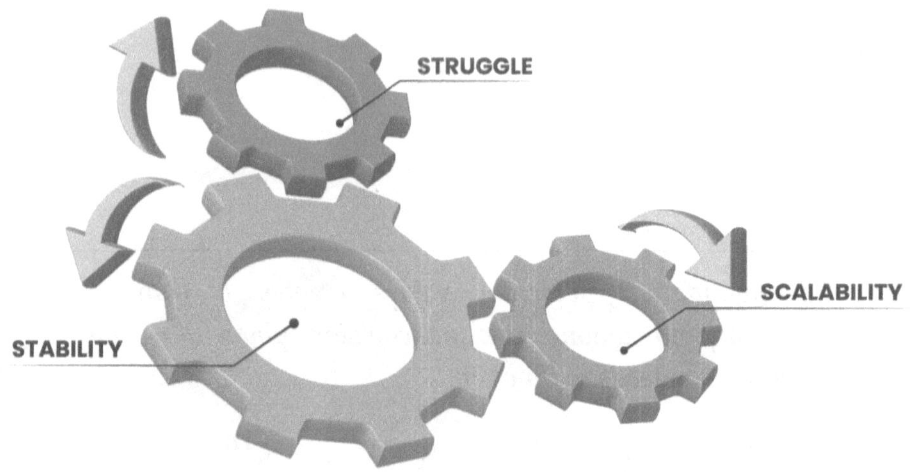

Fig. 2 The Three Phases of the Organization Maturity Cycle

Focus on your organization. What phase is your organization in right now?

Phase 1: Struggle

- You work with a vision.
- You are continuously working and battling with day-to-day objectives, and have a feeling that you need to do it all by yourself. Your perception is either that no one around you is capable, or you have not found the ability in anyone else to execute the task as well as you can.
- It is a chaotic atmosphere at the workplace – either everyone is running, or no one is running.

- Growth is fast but not steady. You see spikes in the financial graphs and you can change gears easily.
- As a leader, you are stressed about the decisions that you make and have a constant feeling of failure.
- Your goals are not specific, and you tend to change them often to achieve the desired outcomes. (The specific chapters will help you understand, learn and implement how to get out of this cycle.)

If you find that your organization is at this stage, you need to invest your time in creating a robust mechanism that will help you craft your future journey with a structured learning process. Scan the QR code below and check out the *Burning Desire Journey*, which can help you in this process.

Fig. 3 QR Code – The Burning Desire Journey

Phase 2: Stability

- Your vision is the same as the one in the Struggle phase.
- Structures in the organization are solidified. Procedures, policies, and standards are well-established.
- Controls and monitoring systems are in place, and standards are being reinforced.
- The management has become more professional and adheres to protocols and procedures.
- Strategizing and planning are done at the top of the pyramid, and the rest of the team follows the instructions.

- People work harder as the management is focusing on sustaining the profits (bottom line and top line) of the business.
- Most importantly, the organization is completely focused on creating efficiency in the system.

Phase 3: Scalability

- This is the stage where leaders and entrepreneurs become extremely restless about their state of being as an organization. During this phase, they decide to revisit the basic purpose of the organization. They want to get back to the drawing board to revisit and imbibe the basic reason for their existence.
- This is where they need to build their mental ability for a leap. This is the time when they need to create their Big Hairy Audacious Goal (BHAG).
- During this phase, leaders challenge the basic assumptions about themselves and the organization; sometimes, even market assumptions are challenged in this phase to forge and craft a new direction for the organization.
- The organization makes wholehearted efforts to reconnect with all its stakeholders with a renewed organizational message, a bigger or better purpose converted into an audacious mission.
- The organization makes an effort to spread a new message across its markets tirelessly.

I recommend that you use the Value Card Method (visit https://siluniversity.com/value-cards or scan the QR code below) to identify your value system, and through a method of questioning and enquiry for yourself and your core team members, find the value system of your organization.

Fig. 4 QR Code – Value Card Method

As a leader, you will be surprised to note that all of your decisions in the past have knowingly or unknowingly been influenced by your values, which also means that if they get into your awareness (Conscious Competence), you will be able to make more educated decisions, thus creating a life and business that are value-based. Successful leaders have operated on a well-guided value system, due to which they were able to create and run their organizations well, which created a long-lasting impression in their fields of operation. Over a period of time, the people who worked with them or for them also knowingly or unknowingly believed in and imbibed those values. Hence, they wholeheartedly supported the leader in the growth of the business or organization. Leaders, managers, and entrepreneurs who focus solely on profits will always get tired mentally as they are focusing on the dynamic aspect of the business. However, leaders who create value-based organizations show signs of growth and prosperity that benefit society at large. These leaders have a clear idea of HOW to create the organization and what kind of decisions they need to make based on the governing principles of their values.

List down your value system that governs your behavior as an entrepreneur and a leader, and define it further. For example,

Value: Integrity

Definition: Do what you say and say what you do

Value: ____

Definition: ____

____

Value: ____

Definition: ____

____

Value: ____

Definition: ____

____

Value: ____

Definition: ____

____

Value: ____

Definition: ____

____

Value: ____

Definition: ____

____

Value: ____

Definition: ____

____

Let us focus on how you can sync your value system with that of your organization.

What are the behavioral aspects (that currently exist) that you would like to encourage continuing in your organization?

____

____

What are the changes in behavior that you need to work on personally that will culminate into a change in people and bring about the desired state in the organization?

____

____

What are the actions you are ready to take to get the required exposure that supports your value system?

____

____

Who are the people who can support your change? (Make a list of those people.)

____

____

What are the three immediate actions you are ready to take that support your organization and your value system?

____

____

> *You must be the change that you want to see in the world.*
>
> *– Mahatma Gandhi*

Understanding How Great Leaders Create Organizations with Effective Personal Rituals

Going beyond the Conscious Competence Learning Model

Great leaders work with people by applying the Conscious Competence Learning Model – a model evolved by Neol Burch in 1970. It is still the most apt model used to build any new skill in people.

My work at SIL (School of Inspirational Leadership) brought me into contact with almost 700+ businesses and 15000+ business leaders globally. I was able to make a significant improvement in their functioning, which lead to profitable, scalable businesses. My observations resulted in the knowledge that while the relevance of the Conscious Competence Learning Model is undeniable, there is a need to look beyond it to achieve results relevant to today's times.

This led me to develop another model, which went much beyond the Conscious Competence Model. It addressed the needs of enterprises today that function in dynamic global environments. It also showed how a leader's consciousness can change the destiny of every stakeholder directly or indirectly attached to the organization. I call this the **"Beyond Conscious Competence Model."** In order to use this this model, we need to understand the following terminology correctly.

Competence – My ability to exhibit my skills with an appropriate set of behaviors demanded by the environment.

Skills – The precision/efficiency of performing an activity.

Behavior – My attributes/approach towards or while performing an activity.

Conscious – My ability to rationalize my surroundings and take the requisite action.

Unconscious – My habituated behaviors, which require minimum or no efforts of rationalization.

Values are the extreme white lines on a highway, which indicate to the driver that crossing those white lines is fatal and will cause accidents.

– Yogesh Pawar

Yogesh's Model – Beyond Conscious Competence

The best leaders of the world who have delivered products and services and have changed the way we live today have gone through the Beyond Conscious Competence Model (knowingly/unknowingly) on a daily basis. The key difference between leaders who *unknowingly* use the Beyond Conscious Competence Model and those who *knowingly* use it is that conscious leaders have complete clarity of what they want to achieve and create. With this, they are completely aware of their actions and their consequences i.e. success or failure. Followers respect their dreams not because they like these leaders but because they see that their dreams will also be fulfilled in this process.

As the Beyond Conscious Competence Model explains, all the stages are part of every leader's DNA that positively and negatively affect the organization or society at large. The model brings out the different styles of leadership. Although each leader has different methods, the objective remains to help and assist teams to produce results that are impacting the marketplace.

Let us read the case study below to understand how this model affects leaders positively and negatively in personal, professional, or social areas where they perform and produce results. Through this case study, you will learn the simplest formula for crafting a *strong value system* for yourself and your organization. On further reading the case, you will realize how your values shape your life unknowingly. And if you are aware of this, your decisions will be far more effective, and you will have immense clarity in your life and business.

But to create value in the organization that you perform in as a leader, you need to understand, comprehend and define your value system.

As leaders, your core strength is being able to take decisions about the aspects that you know of your business or aspects that you don't know of your business. While not taking a decision is also a decision, it may lead to failure, or sometimes, even success. Often, the market calls these decisions the risks of the business, but the organization's ability to take decisions improves when it has leaders who are aware of their and the organization's value systems that act as their internal guidelines or radar for decision-making.

Let us understand the psychological process of how we create methods, beliefs, values, and rituals that drive our present and future as leaders.

Case Study

In 2014, I had undertaken a coaching assignment with Mrs. Shilpa Khanna (name changed), a lady in her mid-forties who was working in a multinational bank in Dubai at a senior position. During a training session, she was struck by a few things through our activities for self-realization. After the session, she expressed her interest in being personally coached on certain challenges that she was facing as a professional and as a woman.

After a week, we met and she started narrating her experiences. "I have been very successful in my professional life, and in the 22 years of my career, I have risen to the top of the organizational pyramid. However, a couple of months ago, when I finished a review, I overheard people saying that I had moved up the ladder by 'managing' various things." I am sure you understand what she meant, and women readers will especially relate to her statement as they too must have heard about or even, for that matter, experienced this at some point in their careers. "This thought that people who work for me, or even above me are thinking about me in this manner is extremely disturbing. In the past, I have heard from people that I am a headstrong woman and that I am powerful enough to get things done. My ex-husband too had said that I am selfish. I could take all that, but I have never done what people are accusing me of, and this has shaken my morale and motivation. It has affected my performance as a leader and as a person."

After listening to her, I asked her a question, "Why are you so disturbed by it? You should ignore it and move on. You are successful in your terms. So, it should hardly matter to you."

She said, "Yogesh, I tried doing that. But the thought that people think me capable of doing such things does not leave my mind."

I asked another question. "Do you feel the issue is with you or the world around you?"

She said, "I feel it's me now because everyone around me, like my ex-husband, colleagues, and juniors, has this perception about me. Today, when I look back, I think that I am unconsciously giving them these experiences through my behavior."

I said, "Would you want to give yourself the commitment to change this?" I was checking if she was sure about her **commitment to change**.

She said, "Yes, I will work on it until I change." That was a promising and assuring answer. I gave her a confirmation of one-on-one sessions where we could discuss this at length and understand the **real causes** behind this situation to accomplish the **real change** that she needed to make.

The next weekend, we met for further discussions. I was even more curious to understand her journey of the last 45 years. It took close to five sessions to understand her entire journey.

I am narrating the essence of this story for you to understand the relevance of the work that was needed to bring about the change.

Shilpa was from a small town near Pune. Her parents were farmers and lived a hand-to-mouth existence. When she was five years old, her brother was born. Although her parents were happy, they were also worried about how they would take care of both children. Shilpa's mother suggested, "My sister is financially well-off and stays in Mumbai. She will be more than happy to take care of Shilpa. We can send Shilpa to her and take care of the little boy here."

Both parents agreed. Shilpa's aunt too agreed to have Shilpa at her place and said that she would take care of her along with her two daughters. While all this was happening, Shilpa, the little five-year-old girl, was observing and listening to everything. She was absolutely unhappy and didn't want to leave her parents. Also, she was hurt due to not being her parents' choice. This made a very strong mark on her mind. She started feeling that she was loved less by her parents. As the time to go to Mumbai came closer, her behavior changed. Her mother noticed this and asked her about it. She started crying, saying that her parents didn't love her anymore and that all their love and attention was for her brother. Her mother explained to her the real reason she was being sent to Mumbai. Shilpa asked her mother a question. "If we have a lot of money, will we be able to stay together?"

Her mother affirmed with a "Yes." **[Notice what the mother affirmed.]** Slowly but steadily, Shilpa's mother was able to pacify her. After two months, she went to Mumbai. Although this was painful for her, little Shilpa was mesmerized by Mumbai. As she went to school with her cousins, she made a promise to herself that she would earn a lot of money and one day, get her family back together. **[Notice what she affirmed to herself as a result of this incident and the reason behind it.]**

As days passed, Shilpa began to enjoy her school life, which she wouldn't have been able to in her hometown. Her aunt had two little girls, her cousins, who used to go to school with her. Shilpa's uncle and aunt were working professionals, and both managed their finances well. However, there were many instances when Shilpa had to let go of small but important demands/requests **[according to her]** as the unconscious preference was given to her cousins.

Every time this happened, she used to work harder in school and invest more time in her studies just to ensure that if she scored well, she would be able to get a job and support her needs. When she used to be alone, she affirmed that she would earn a lot of money so that her family and she would always be able to get whatever they wanted. **[Note what she reinforced.]**

With the motivation to achieve financial freedom, she excelled in her studies and topped each class. She also achieved a scholarship for her university studies and was praised by everyone including her uncle, aunt, parents, and teachers. Her confidence was at its peak. Her performance was very often compared to that of her cousins, and it was suggested that they learn from her. As days passed, she became an example for the people around her. She told me, "I used to love competing with my classmates. It gave me pleasure to win and be praised. I wanted to do it more often." **[Mark what Shilpa wanted to do more often and how the significance of being noticed had started creeping into her mind.]**

Slowly but steadily, competing and winning became a habit, which was infused with a strong feeling of significance. After she completed her studies, she was offered a job by a multinational bank. "This was a dream come true for me," she said. "It took me back to those days when I had to leave my parents. Now, I knew I could get them back." She put her heart and soul into her work. The results were the same she excelled at whatever she did. She once again loved the professional competition and the result **[money and recognition]** that she was getting out of it.

Organizations love employees who are high achievers. Such employees climb the corporate ladder faster than others, and that's what happened with Shilpa as well. In ten years, she was appointed the head of a small unit of the bank, which intended to focus on retail banking. She was given complete liberty to achieve results and had a free hand in managing resources. By this time, the top management had seen a future leader in her. Hence, they motivated her to do her best.

This was a great high in her career. She pushed herself and the entire team and led from the front. She took tough decisions to make things happen. During this time, she had already become someone who could single-handedly take over any team and make them perform. Her decisions were final, and she only accepted "Yes, Boss!" behavior from the employees.

On the personal front, her parents had already shifted to a huge apartment in Mumbai, and her younger brother had started attending college. Everyone was proud of Shilpa.

During the journey, she had changed tremendously. She had now become very demanding in her approach, and her decisions were to be accepted by everyone without any deviation. She truly believed that what she did generated profits for the bank. Hence, there was no scope for any other input from anyone. Several managers and senior managers were working with her. It was clear to them that it was "her way or the highway." By now, she had become very influential with the top management. However, her subordinates called her "Hitler." Shilpa was aware of this tag that she had acquired. Her core team, who were now her good friends, often used to say, "How can it be your way or the highway?" She used to smirk and say, "The boss is always right!" **[During our sessions, she agreed that she loved that power and authority.]**

On the personal side too, changes were happening. Manav, her college friend, proposed to her, and they decided to get married. Manav was a level-headed guy and knew how Shilpa had carved her niche in the corporate world. He was aware that he was marrying a self-driven, headstrong girl who had a great fighting spirit and never took no for an answer.

On the work side, Shilpa performed well both individually and as a leader. She had become one of the top influential people in the bank. She told me that she aspired to become the CEO. She was quickly marching towards this goal of hers, but now, people around her were seeing a different Shilpa – a person with a domineering attitude who controlled everything that came under her purview of work and influenced every stakeholder that needed to be persuaded.

The newly-married couple hardly had time for each other. Manav was a little more reasonable and understood why Shilpa was so focused on work. Three years later, Shilpa had two great announcements to make – she was finally the CEO of the bank, and was also about to deliver a baby. A couple of months later, Rohan was born. The entire family was extremely happy.

Manav, who ran his own business, took time out for Rohan. It was difficult for Shilpa to do so as her life revolved around the bank and the enormous responsibilities that she was handling. As Rohan grew up, he would always complain, "Dad is always around me, but you are never there!" There were frequent arguments between Manav and Shilpa on this issue. She narrated, "It was not that I didn't want to spend time with Rohan or Manav, but I was handling a lot of responsibility and was at a very senior position, and couldn't let go of what I had achieved with a lot of passion and zeal." **[Mark that she didn't want to let go.]**

Her travel and work always kept her from spending time with Rohan and Manav. The biggest mistake she made was forgetting their tenth wedding anniversary. Manav lost it this time, and the argument led to such chaos that they decided to separate. Then started the clash of egos and the process of justifying how Shilpa was right. She had done it all for all of them, and especially for Rohan. Finally, Rohan and Manav moved out, and Shilpa started staying alone in her big apartment. However, she never felt it was completely her fault because she believed that she was right. After all, she had always been right. **[Mark what she now believed.]**

Shilpa was moving through life at a fast pace. She had left behind her parents, her brother, husband, and son – ironically, for the very reasons she had wanted to become a CEO in the first place. Until that day, when she overheard people say that everyone knew how she had reached the top!

She said, "That shook me. I lost my confidence, and started believing that I was alone." Hence, she started working harder and was tougher on the people around her as she wanted to be seen as a tough lady who could manage challenges of any sort.

I am sure that you, as readers, have noticed the changes that occurred in Shilpa's journey from starting alone to ending up alone. We will now analyze what went wrong, whether she or the environment was to blame and whether she or the people around her were victims. Let's go step by step.

1. Shilpa was appreciated for the results that she achieved, and was rewarded and recognized for the way she functioned. *However, her reason for achieving the results was never observed. It was the fear of being alone again that drove her to ruthlessly achieve it all.*

2. *Every time she did well, she was affirming subconsciously that that was the way to get results.* The problem began when she started expecting the people around her, her brother, her parents, uncle, aunt, cousins, subordinates, and husband to behave the same way as she did because she believed that it was the right way.

3. *She got the right results for the wrong reasons.* Let us ask some questions here:

Did she earn enough money?	– Yes
Did she buy a big house?	– Yes
Was she able to get her family back together?	– Yes
Did she achieve power, authority, and recognition?	– Yes
Was she happy?	– A big NO!

Let us understand Shilpa's behaviors and how she created methods, beliefs, values, and rituals that drove her as a leader.

- A **thought** of not wanting to be alone was implanted in her mind at the beginning.

- Her **observations** started creating **assumptions** about how things should be done and her **actions** were based on them.
- This became her **natural way of functioning**.
- Her natural way of functioning was **repeatedly supported the environment**.
- Due to **external reinforcement,** her natural **actions** were converted into **habits**.
- Her **habits** got converted into **beliefs, due to repetition**.
- These **beliefs** made her **expect** the same **behavior** from the people around her in various environments. However, her behavior was only appreciated professionally.
- When people in the environment started following her **behavior**, it became a strong **perceived value** in her.
- A **value system** like independence drove her to act independently and as a result, being correct and ambitious became a part of her **rituals**.

(All these observations are relevant only to this case. This may not be true for everyone because although two leaders may have the same value, its definition will differ in the case of each leader.)

You may wonder why I have narrated a negative experience to demonstrate the working of the Beyond Conscious Competence Model, rather than a positive one. This is purely because once the problem is diagnosed right, one can change a negative experience into a positive one.

Successful leaders know for sure what values and rituals they want to imbibe in themselves and the organizations they serve, consciously avoiding the trap of negative reinforcement of the environment. Hence, they begin with the core values and what they mean to them and derive a well-crafted vision. Leaders come from various cultures, financial states, castes, creeds, and religions. However, every leader has a value system that drives him/her. It is like their personal guide or the internal radar that helps them navigate through every process of decision-making, personally and professionally.

Great leaders realize the power of the environment to drive the organization's culture and focus on creating a culture within the organization that is hopeful, engaged, happy, and focused, irrespective of any external stimuli. It is imperative that you, as a leader, realize this today and create those value-based guidelines to help you take that big leap in your organization. A **Value** is, "A timeless guiding principle that requires no external justification."

While the definition above says "no external justification," it means that once the value has been decided by the leaders in the organization, has cascaded down, and is agreed to by everyone in the organization, it does not need any external market justification. These are organizations that operate inside-out rather than outside-in. Many leaders believe in the outside-in philosophy. However, it is important to realize that if your organization is not driven inside-out, it will lose the essence of being persistent in difficult times. The very reason for the organization's existence will be questioned, leaving the employees directionless. In the future, the organization shall reach a position where people have lost faith in the internal system. These value systems need to be driven through various processes and actions throughout the organization. They should reflect into the products and services that your organization provides at the marketplace.

Whether it is a personal value or an organizational value, leaders first need to realize the value, define it and tirelessly communicate it down to the very bottom of the organizational pyramid. Once this is accomplished, these leaders empower their transactional or tactical leaders or the middle management to take effective decisions. The workforce always works within the safety and growth parameters of performance, usually called Key Performance Areas (KPA).

In the world of disruption and ever-changing technology where products and services are changing every day, every company is looking for a bigger piece of the consumer mindshare and pocket share to enhance its profits. Moreover, startups come up with disruptive ideas and kill the market share of bigger companies. However, if you observe closely, not more than ten percent of startups really grow into big corporations. Two of the core reasons for this are:

1. Lack of a compelling vision for the future, and
2. The lack of a robust value system for the organization that they are building, and the discipline required during the execution process.

Core values need to be converted into operating principles, which become rules for daily decision-making in the company. If the vision, values and daily decision-making processes are not aligned with the Big Hairy Audacious Goal, then this leads to a drop in the motivation of the employees, poor cash flows, bad customer service, delays in deliveries, personal conflicts among team members and attrition, ultimately leading to the fall of the company.

As a preacher or believer of this philosophy, I recommend that leaders establish and follow a strong value system within themselves and the organization. What you want to achieve and how you want to achieve it, is a result of what your values are. Once your values and what you want to achieve are defined, what remains is to chalk out a process acceptable to all the stakeholders.

While doing this, leaders are often distracted and get carried away by external triggers because they need to create an immediate impact in the dynamic marketplace. However, great leaders realize that the journey always is and always has to be driven inside-out.

The Seven Stages of Building Organizational Rituals

Understanding the model of driving an organization inside-out will help you create a sustainable business and long-lasting profits by using the **Beyond Conscious Competence Model**. This requires a leader to build sound and lasting Organizational Rituals. Here are the seven stages in which this can be done.

Stage 1: Realizing the Core Values

- Aligning personal values with the organization's values and creating a simple definition of each value, which acts as a guiding principle for decision-making at all levels of the organization.
- Defining/redefining the organization's purpose gives a clear indication to employees at all levels about what and how they need to work in order to be aligned with the organization's value systems.
- Cascading the core value system throughout the organization through various communication channels repeatedly.
- Creating value champions who are naturally inclined towards and who believe in the organization's value system, and can demonstrate it through regular operational activities.
- Creating monitoring systems that are non-threatening, which allows people to fail in the process of adopting the value system. However, the organization should make them responsible for correcting failures and appreciate their contribution to their work.
- Creating a reward mechanism for every individual who displays the value and fits into the agreed definition.

Stage 2: Creating a Big Goal

- This is a goal that looks difficult, but if achieved, can change the fate of the organization and the people working for it.

- Successful leaders persuade people in the organization and help them to continuously visualize this big goal.[1]

Stage 3: Strategy

- Create a strategic roadmap, which aligns the organization with its big goal.
- The big goal needs to be created and aligned with every department of the organization. Employees need a vision (a picture of the future) and an understanding of their new state of being in the organization. This one task will get the team motivated to move forward every day.
- As mentioned earlier in the chapter, the value system is like a guideline to decision-making that helps employees and leaders in an organization to make decisions at all levels.
- In the process of building a certain ecosystem, there will be employees, leaders, or even partners of the organization who will be dissatisfied. An open dialogue is needed with them, and a complete attempt at alignment needs to be made with the dissatisfied employees, or else, they may cause fatal resistance in the change process.
- **Caution:** Do take care of them well. There is a process explained in the later chapters on how to deal with difficult people during the change process.
- A clear focus must be established at the product level, service level, customer level, process level and system level, which will bring in a leap in the business if it serves the market well. This requires minute-level planning to be done by the head of the organization along with his core team.

---

1   NOTE - Decide this big goal along with your core team and all the positive believers in decision-making roles.

Stage 4: Projects

- Operational and strategic priorities aligned to the vision and mission of the organization are important aspects when you create internal developmental or revenue-generating projects for the teams. These projects need to be aligned with the business strategy and treated accordingly.
- People in the organization need to be rewarded and recognized at regular intervals during the change process of implementing the **Seven Stages of Building Organizational Rituals.** The leaders need to build a transparent reward and recognition system that helps the employees stay motivated and move forward in the chosen direction.
- During the operating levels of the strategic change initiative, the organization needs to build a tracking system for resources (man, machine, and method) development. The tracking mechanism could give predictive results of process improvement, system improvement, and most importantly, skill and competency improvement of employees. At certain stages, employees will be realigned, retrained, re-coached, or replaced as per the priorities of the organization.

Stage 5: Guidelines

- Creating a list of rules and guidelines to achieve results. This is a dynamic set of actions that leaders need to create and review at regular intervals. Analogically, these are the levers of change management, which need to be monitored through a system like ERP or CRM, which helps the organization achieve results.
- Creating a Behavior Competency Framework, which in simple terms, means guidelines about "How People Should Behave" when they are executing a task themselves, or with each other on a daily basis.
- Creating a learning roadmap for all key stakeholders and the relevant business projects that they need to implement.

- Your role as the leader or an entrepreneur of your ecosystem is to monitor the processes correctly and constantly find opportunities to repeat the value systems in various forms in the organization. One more major task is to take care of people. Remember – monitor the processes and take care of people.

Stage 6: Infrastructure

- It is the leader's job to create the infrastructure that is conducive to producing the change results. This includes arranging for the requirements of space, various technology support systems, hardware requirements, perks, human resource and performance policies that are required for people to perform, and many more.

Stage 7: Results

- A crisp monitoring system of processes to be followed needs to be in place. The art is getting your core team to accept it. Hence, it has to be created with the involvement of the various leaders of the organization. This kind of approach will help you drive new results for the organization constantly. People will be motivated to work as they are constantly chasing and achieving targets that they set for themselves.

- Results are the output. Successful leaders attempt to make the approach to the results simple and constantly observe and coach teams on achieving the output through the right inputs. This is the stage when successful leaders change their stance from not just being leaders of the organization but also being wonderful coaches to drive results. Note that your personal behavior is a big part of your coaching as a leader; you cannot preach what you don't practice. However, there will be instances when you are not able to practice what you preach. Make sure you are open to your people about this and seek their assistance to help you achieve the goal. This displays your strength as a leader –

to be humble enough to accept the aspects that you have not been able to execute successfully, and ask your subordinates for their suggestions and help. Being upfront and honest are important traits of successful leaders from any walk of life.

Exercise:

Refer the Beyond Conscious Competence Model and answer the questions below.

S. No.	Actions	For Yourself	For your Team
1.	What are the conscious skills you want to develop to be competent?		
2.	What is the knowledge you want to develop consciously to improve competence?		
3.	What is the one behavior you want to promote personally and in the organization?		
4.	What is the environment you intend to create to build your competence?		

Choose Actions that are aligned with your Vision, Mission, Values, and Strategy.

To Summarize:

> - Decide what kind of habits, values, beliefs, and rituals you want the organization to be driven by.
> - Understand that repeated information in various forms creates a belief in people.
> - People with a common belief create a culture and establish norms to live and perform.
> - Environment and time are two critical factors that drive an organization's value system.
> - Monitor processes and systems. Take care of people.
> - Constantly forming newer objectives will help leaders drive long-term results.
> - Communicate honestly with people.

NOTES:

Your interpretation of this chapter: Every leader has his own way of looking at a particular concept. Writing your interpretation of this chapter below will help make it relevant to your life. Creating relevance will add clarity. You can be descriptive while writing your interpretation.

For example, you may write – After understanding the Beyond Conscious Competence Model, I understand that the belief system that I had created in my childhood may be irrelevant today, and hence, I intend to change it.

Learnings that you will implement: Ask yourself what you have learned and how you will use these learnings in your professional life.

____

____

____

____

____

____

____

____

____

____

____

____

____

____

CHAPTER 2

CREATING EFFICIENT ORGANIZATIONS

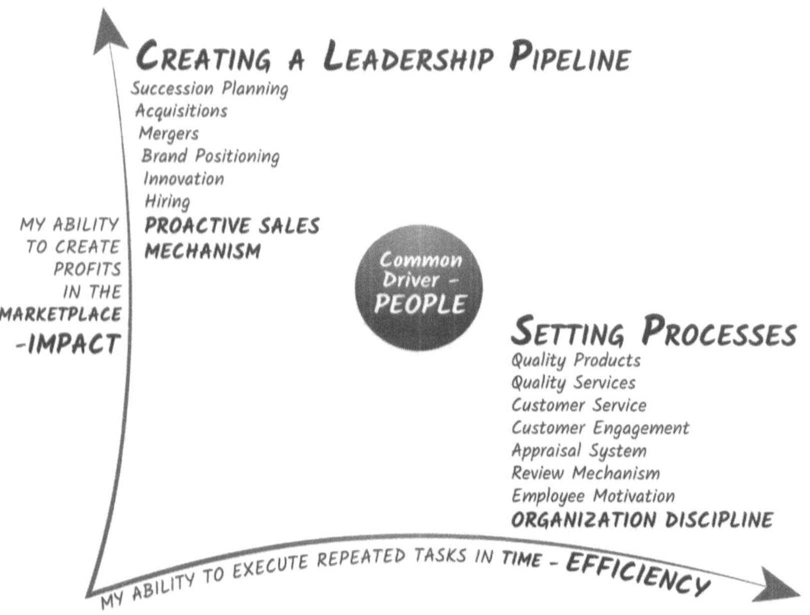

Fig. 5 Impact vs. Efficiency

Note: This chapter focuses on the X axis of the graph – Creating efficient organizations. We shall see how to create an impact (Y axis of the graph) in Chapter 3.

The above model helps us understand how great leaders operate.

All efficiency-level activities are created and managed by efficient people hired by the organization. These activities are not undertaken by successful leaders but are initiated and handed over to the transactional leaders of the organization. This is what I call "creating" an efficient, future-ready organization, where the organization has complete control over its processes, discipline, systems, methods, and rewards.

In order to create an efficient organization, successful leaders plan "smart goals" that connect and bind people together to perform repetitive tasks (for example, sales or servicing customers) efficiently. Successful leaders motivate and engage their efficient employees to do the same activities consistently and persistently. Efficiency in people, systems, and methods creates an organization that is ready to take the next leap. Successful leaders understand the tipping point and anticipate when to go full throttle to create a market impact.

In this chapter, you will enhance your knowledge about how to choose methods, processes, systems, people, and relevant tools to create an efficient organization.

Successful leaders choose people who are aligned with the **value system** of the organization. They ensure that the right people with the correct cultural fit, behaviors, and the ability to demonstrate those behaviors at the workplace, are chosen.

During the selection processes, leaders make sure that the **organization's value system** and **organizational vision** are adhered to in the processes and systems that they have built. As mentioned, efficiency is always about tuning four things: Man, Machine, Method, and Material.

Great leaders use organizational values as the foundation stone, and grounding principles for other leaders and employees to work on.

Creating an Efficient Workforce by Organizing Repetitive Tasks – What I term the Delegation Matrix

In order to create an efficient workforce, you, as a leader, must start focusing on the repetitive tasks that are performed in your organization. This works in seven stages.

- Step 1: Identification of repetitive tasks
- Step 2: Segregation of repetitive tasks
- Step 3: Alignment of repetitive tasks
- Step 4: Assigning the repetitive tasks
- Step 5: Delegating the repetitive tasks
- Step 6: Monitoring the repetitive tasks
- Step 7: Rewarding the performance of repetitive tasks

Let us get a step-by-step understanding of each stage.

➢ **Step 1: Identification of Repetitive Tasks**

Try answering this question.

What are the tasks in your organization/department/role that "Must be done?" List them now.

____

____

____

➢ **Step 2: Segregation of Repetitive Tasks**

You have made a list of the "Must do" tasks in your earlier answer.

Let us segregate those tasks into the following categories:

i.   Tasks that can be handled by machine/software

____

____

____

____

____

ii.   Tasks that can be managed by processes

____

____

____

____

____

iii.   Tasks that require people's intervention

____

____

____

____

____

What are the developmental tasks that help you work better? For example, training programs, building CFTs – Cross-functional Teams, etc.

____

____

____

____

____

You have thus segregated the tasks and identified the activities or tasks that you will not perform yourself, but for which, you will put systems, processes, or people in place. You have also identified tasks that will help you improve the performance of people.

➢   **Step 3: Alignment of Repetitive Tasks**

What are the interconnecting tasks where you are sure that if task X is not done, then task Y will not happen? The arrows denote the Lead and Lag between each task.

__________ ←——→ __________

__________ ←——→ __________

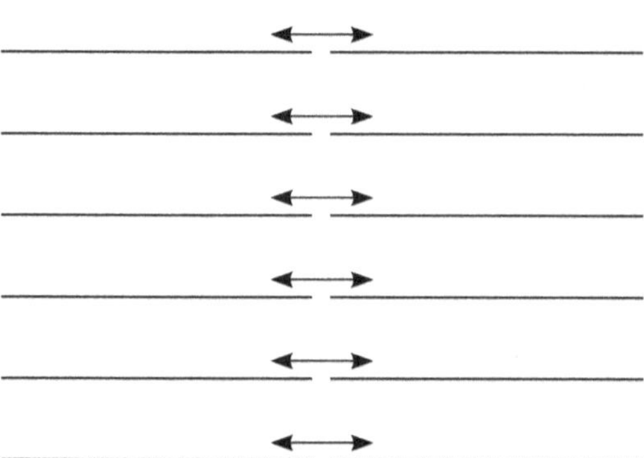

Do not pick up more than eight activities because you will neither be able to focus on all of them nor execute them.

➢ **Step 4: Assigning the Repetitive Tasks**

Who are the people (internal/external) that you believe can perform the tasks mentioned in the above question?

Name	Level	Task

Level Legend:

- Level 1: The person has to be informed about the task
- Level 2: The person has to be monitored
- Level 3: The person has to be assigned the task and rewarded for performance

➢ **Step 5: Delegating the Repetitive Tasks**

Who are the people you can give authority to in your organization at the levels mentioned below?

Level 5 (Complete authority of decision-making)

Level 4 (Operational authority of decision-making)

Level 3 (Transactional authority of decision-making)

Level 2 (Specific authority of decision-making)

Level 1 (No authority)

You can have more than one person at each level.

Level	Name	Task
Level 5		
Level 4		
Level 3		
Level 2		
Level 1		

If you have more people at Level 5, your organization is at the right stage of scalability and growth.

If you have more people at Level 1, you are more of a sophisticated, self-employed professional who enjoys power and authority and may not know the right method to leverage people and time. (Sorry if I hurt your ego; but it's true!)

However, you can change this immediately. One of the methods of balancing the organization is called the **Balanced Score Card** in which, learning & development, internal impact, external impact and shareholder impact can be measured on a regular basis. Scan the QR code below to access my video on the Balanced Score Card.

Fig. 6 QR Code – Balanced Score Card

> **Step 6: Monitoring the Repetitive Tasks**

What are the ways that can help you understand whether the repeated tasks are being performed efficiently?

Example: Creating a monthly dashboard, which motivates a Sales team to perform better.

Make a list of viable methods that need to be created for daily, weekly, and monthly monitoring of repeated tasks.

➢ **Step 7: Rewarding the Performance of Repetitive Tasks**

What benefits are you willing to give your people who perform the repeated tasks within the given time and by meeting quality standards?

____

____

____

____

What benefits are you ready offer to those who you have delegated the task to and who are monitoring it for you?

____

____

____

____

With this simple seven-step process, you will be able to create an efficient and impactful workforce that drives productivity within the organization and profits in the marketplace. The important elements that you as a leader need to acquire, are the **ability and quality to engage the workforce and keep them motivated to do the same job efficiently.** Employee satisfaction surveys across the globe are treated with respect and taken seriously because an engaged and motivated workforce is a productive workforce.

The Core of Human Motivation

Fig. 7 The Core of Human Motivation

At the core of employee motivation, lie the three basic human values of

1. Autonomy (Desire of people to run their own lives)
2. Mastery (To continuously keep doing their work better), and
3. Purpose (Doing everything they do at the workplace with a reason)

The outer three layers in the diagram are those of elements visible in the behaviors and actions of employees, which can be influenced by the leader in order to achieve the desired vision.

1. Emotional Triggers
2. Systems to Support, and
3. Agile and Rewarding Processes

Let us understand them better.

1. **Emotional Triggers** – If money is not the issue, what are the other things that motivate you at your workplace? If you are able to identify this for yourself, you will be able to identify this for your employees too.

____

____

____

____

____

Let us focus on these things to engage your employees.

Let us take a look at the eight drivers, other than money, that drive humans, to engage in a productive workforce. The following list is derived from Arthur F. Carmazzi's Emotional Drivers of Performance and David McClelland's Theory of Motivation:

- Achievement – Their innate need to achieve goals
- Challenge – Their innate need of getting into unknowns
- Diversity – Their innate need of doing or experiencing new things
- Love/Belongingness – Their innate need of feeling ownership of what they have or what they want, along with togetherness
- Significance – Their innate need of being noticed and recognized by others
- Control – Their innate need for feeling secure in every situation or with people
- Excellence – Their innate need of reaching the pinnacle of everything that they do
- Contribution – Their innate need for giving

- These are the internal and external triggers that humans receive from their environment. Great leaders create an environment of positive triggers that create a productive environment.

These dynamic drivers need to be used in alignment with the organization's vision and mission. For example, if the focus is on innovation, then, give employees a day in a quarter free from organizational priorities and allow them to focus on what they enjoy innovating. This is a good way to engage them.

Keeping in mind the dynamic nature of business, leaders create an environment of safety, belongingness, and control, which enhances collaborative working, empathy, transparency, and creativity at the workplace.

2. **Systems to Support** – This refers to creating an engaging system that is easy to use and provides people with triggers to complete their tasks in time. For example, a content writer using a copywriting tool that allows him to get options for various subjects. Also, a payroll system that automates the repetitive task of payrolls or an invoicing system that gives reminders to your customers to pay on time.

3. **Agile and Rewarding Processes** – When you want to achieve certain things, you need to set processes. However, the processes that a leader sets cannot be rigid. He must create agile processes that help people reach their objectives. This is because people have their ways of doing things as well. For example, a hybrid mode of working in the new VUCA world, where employees are ready to work from home as well as from the office.

To create an efficient organization, we need these three layers in place. After studying Figure 7, you will realize that at the core are the Values, for example, Autonomy, Mastery and Purpose, which can be defined differently for different organizations, and as employees shift from one organization to another, they carry the different value definitions of their old organizations or the environment they come from. However, great leaders understand that they have to define what Autonomy, Mastery and Purpose mean in their organizations in order to create an efficient culture that positively impacts the marketplace.

> *As a leader, you take care of the small things that matter to the right people and they will take care of the big things in the organization.*
>
> *— Yogesh Pawar*

How to Drive Change to Create an Efficient Organization

Here are the actions that you, as a leader, need to take for driving change that will result in creating an efficient organization. It is not necessary that all the people in the organization will accept this change that you intend to induce. Adoption of this new thought process is the biggest change that you as a leader need to focus on. People have fears, and they are fearful of change because they don't see the future as you do. Instead, they focus on how this change shall create inconvenience in their work life. Once you have the new processes written down and your Delegation Matrix (described at the beginning of this chapter) is done correctly, here are the things you "must do" as a leader:

1. **Improve your Hiring Efficiency**

You have to find the right people for the right jobs and then let them get things done. Let us look at some traits based on which we will hire people. They must be good team players, should be able to make tactical decisions on the field if the subordinates have queries, must be self-motivated to drive sales numbers, should understand the needs of the industry and work accordingly, should be excited about the job to be done, and be willing to share knowledge and coach their subordinates.

2. **Clarify what you Expect and keep Repeating it**

This process starts even before you hire a person. First, write down your expectation and validate it with your business requirement. Once you have the person on board, make sure that you complete the expectation-setting exercise with the individual within 48 hours of him/her joining the company. This expectation-setting can be divided into two aspects.

- Part 1 – "WHAT" you as leader expect from the individual, and
- Part 2 – "HOW" you expect him/her to behave while delivering the result

For example, if I hire a Sr. Manager - Production, one expectation that I would have as a leader is that the daily plant performance dashboard should be circulated to all the relevant stakeholders before 10 am (This is the "WHAT" part of the job). Secondly, the Sr. Manager needs to get along with everyone and get the report from the relevant stakeholders in time. (So, "Interpersonal Skills" is the "HOW" part of the job.) Likewise, you need to set the expectation of each aspect of the job with the individual hired. The same exercise needs to be done with the existing team as well.

> *Your expectations are the inputs of employees performance.*
> *If they don't perform, the ownership lies with you.*
>
> *— Yogesh Pawar*

3. Set Realistic Goals

I am sure that you must have heard of the stretched goals that leaders tend to give their teams. These leaders are often confused between stretched goals and realistic goals. Realistic goals are goals that are doable, that make people happy and help them to be creatively constructive in the process of achieving them. On the other hand, if people are given stretched targets or goals, they have to focus so much on achieving them that they lose the balance between their personal and professional lives. It is important for a leader to understand this mechanism and set people up for success. When you have a large number of people happily working towards realistic goals, this has a compounding positive effect on the organization.

> *Time creates urgency and emotions create persistence. This is the secret of Goal Setting.*
>
> *— Yogesh Pawar*

4. Let your People be the Problem Solvers. You be the Guide

Continuously train your staff to create solutions to the problems or challenges that the marketplace creates for them. Most of the time, entrepreneurs or leaders tend to give solutions to their team members to avoid time lags while executing their work. This behavior of the entrepreneur or leader stops the development of his subordinates or employees. As a result, the employees are always dependent on them and their decisions, and never feel confident about solving problems themselves. One of the finest solutions that I have practiced and preached is peer-to-peer coaching, which allows the employee to take relevant risks in the marketplace. In Chapter 4, a robust mechanism to handle this situation has been given under the heading, **The Top Five Qualities that Help Leaders Explore the Endless Possibilities of Growth and Profitability through People.**

The wonderful leaders that I have personally worked with, went one step further and asked me to come up with the solution first and then tell them the problem. This made me confident about the decisions that I had taken in my professional life and allowed me to fail and bounce back.

I always play a game with my reportees by asking them relevant questions. This game is played in an enjoyable way that makes them feel comfortable to brainstorm and allows their creative intelligence to work while solving a problem or seeking an opportunity. To give you an example of how it works, I will narrate an incident during the early years of my career. One of the challenges that I faced in my professional life was the utility of a software that was created for better efficiency. I knew well that I could not go to my leader with the problem of the software not being adopted by mass users in the company. Hence, I needed to have a solution *before* I walked into his cabin. So, two days prior, I worked out a plan, which encouraged the users to use the software through a gamified method and point system. I created various parameters where the user would gain points for using the software and for the duration for which the software was used.

When I walked into my leader's cabin, I proposed a solution and explained the problem to him. What he had to do was either say yes or give me an alternative to work with. My leader was pleased to know that I had already worked out a solution and was happy to see the creative angle that I had developed for the adoption of the software. I give him complete credit for creating this mindset among most of my peers and me. Even today, when I am faced with a problem or challenge personally or professionally, I automatically start looking for solutions and now, in the role of a leader and a businessman, I have been able to cultivate the same mindset in my people. The key is to train your staff regularly and allow *them* to propose solutions to the challenges that they face in the marketplace.

Regular training can give them exposure in their professional life and is the only toolkit that they use while solving high-risk business issues. Giving them the opportunity to learn through training, projects, and business challenges is the only way to make an efficient organization where people are hundred percent sure of their abilities.

> *If you think training is a cost to the company, just sit back and calculate the cost of untrained people!*
>
> *– Yogesh Pawar*

5. Hold Effective and Focused Meetings

Long meetings are the biggest time wasters in a company. They exhaust you with either less or no productivity. We have all been to those meetings that drag on, where people ramble, agendas are not defined, meetings move away from the agendas, there is a lack of correct information and insufficient notice for preparation.

As leaders, when you hold meetings, make them worth the time you invest. Decide the meeting in advance and also what the objectives of the meeting are. A meeting should only have five purposes:

- For the collective problem to be solved
- To impart relevant information
- To collectively and intelligently brainstorm
- To make decisions
- To appoint responsible and accountable people to execute the decision

All meetings may not fulfill all the five purposes. For example, you have made a decision, and have called the meeting only to pass on the information to your staff. Once you enter the meeting room, inform the people about it, answer questions, dispel doubts and close the meeting. Make sure that your time and theirs is respected.

> *Never give your audience the perception that your meetings are unnecessarily lengthy with no actions to drive them.*
>
> *— Yogesh Pawar*

6. Create a feeling of Oneness for the Right Reasons

Your employees are human. They come to work with you to get paid. What do they do with their salaries? They buy houses, cars, insurance, schooling for their children and all the things that they and their families need, which make them more secure and socially accepted. They like challenges, and deep down, they want to be successful at their work. They want to be a part of the bigger story, but they don't realize how they can. A successful leader understands that the money an employee is paid is the output of the time and skills he rents out to the company. Hence, if you want ordinary people to perform extraordinary tasks, you need to bind them to an emotion or cause, create a sense of belonging, and then let them do their jobs.

Caution: As a leader, first you need to be sure that you are completely convinced about the cause because your conviction will reflect in everything you do as well as in the instructions you give your staff.

We have ample examples in corporate, social or political history where people coming together with a single emotion have changed the course of the social ecosystem.

> *Bind people with common emotions and see them perform extraordinarily.*
>
> *– Yogesh Pawar*

7. Promote Loyalty and Togetherness

When you promote loyalty towards the organization, and team members, you make sure that you are taking care of people for the long-term. As leaders, you spend more time with your teammates than with your family. Well, your team is also a family. They look up to you when you display loyalty. With the spirit to work together binding the team, you will get the well-deserved respect. Can you do this on a daily basis in your work life? The answer is YES!

You will have to do all of this at regular intervals with your people. Healthy behaviors like (PEARL) Proactivity, Engagement, Appreciation, Recognition and Listening are to be made a part of your daily operations as a leader. These behaviors which have been explained in a later chapter, are the magic behaviors that will inspire people to be like you, and most importantly, to succeed as leaders.

> *Make sure you inspire your team with your actions, and not only your words.*
>
> *– Yogesh Pawar*

To Summarize:

Before creating an **Impact** at the marketplace, do focus on creating an **Efficient Organization.** It is not only about growing but also about sustaining the growth. Delegation plays a key role in creating an efficient organization. People are the only resources that can multiply your emotions manifold. Hence a committed workforce that is delegated the right tasks and is excited to perform, can create miracles for an organization.

Entrepreneurs who create scalable organizations, always focus on creating a culture that is sustainable and scalable. These entrepreneurs always drive the motivation behind the change in the organization. They have the ability to help their teams visualize bigger, better and a larger future that is successful. And hence, at the core of any success lies the motivation of a better future.

Here's how to drive Change in the organization –

- Improve your hiring efficiency
- Clarify what you expect and keep repeating it
- Set realistic goals
- Let your people be the problem solvers. You be the guide.
- Hold effective and focused meetings
- Create a feeling of oneness
- Promote loyalty and togetherness

NOTES:

Your interpretation of this chapter:

Learnings that you will implement:

CHAPTER 3

How Successful Founders Create Impactful Organizations

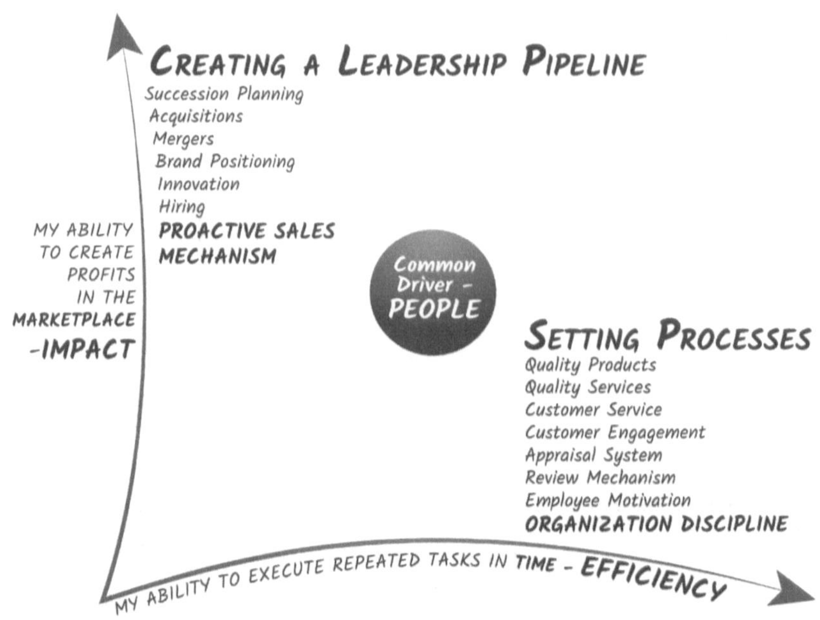

Fig. 8 Impact vs. Efficiency

In Chapter 2, we discussed the X axis of the graph – Creating efficient organizations. In this chapter, we shall discuss the Y-axis – Impact – a leader's ability to create profits in the marketplace.

This model has evolved and been applied for over a number of years now, and shows common patterns of what successful leaders have done in political, social or entrepreneurial journeys. Let us understand the word "IMPACT." The dictionary meaning of the word "IMPACT" is, "the action of one object coming into contact with another." From a business point of view, what happens to your product or service when it comes in contact with the marketplace? It could be constructive and world-changing, or it could also be an absolute failure.

Right now, as you are working in an organization or running your business, ask yourself, "What are the actions in my organization or in my role that I need to take, which are obvious?" They should be legally and logically acceptable in the marketplace. List them down.

I recommend you to have at least ten items, which are (obviously) legal in your business and can generate a profitable impact at the marketplace.

____

____

____

____

____

____

____

____

If all of them have been implemented, push yourself to make a new list of things that have not been implemented yet.

____

____

____

____

____

____

Once you have this list, ask yourself what has stopped you from implementing these tasks. Choose from the reasons mentioned below:

1. You did not focus on them
2. You did not know about them
3. You were busy with something else
4. You were procrastinating

Whatever the reason, you can put down dates by which you will get these activities done.

If you have put the dates, ask yourself:

What are the emotional benefits that I will get by achieving or implementing these activities?

____

____

____

Which relationships will be positively affected by their implementation? Personal/professional?

____

____

____

Executing these activities will help you take a big leap towards scalability. Remember to follow the law of the land while doing so. Understand what is within the laws applicable to your business so that you make no mistakes that you cannot repair. The next big thing that successful leaders focus on is what is logical in the marketplace – understanding trends, anticipating change and making employees aware and focused about the future. **The principle is that the marketplace is always demanding something – a product or service which is BETTER, FASTER, CHEAPER and EASIER.** Hence, predictive, logical and constructive debates need to be encouraged by the leader in the organization. A leader needs to challenge the status quo at regular intervals.

Definitions:

Better: A product or service that can be understood well by the consumer. This could be through its features or look and feel.

Faster: A product or service that can be accessed swiftly by the consumer. For example, due to its quick availability. But, it has to be quicker than it was in the past.

Cheaper: A product or service that is more cost-effective than it was in the past.

Easier: A product or service that is easily understood by the end consumer. This could be due to its adaptability or usability at the marketplace.

Just imagine you and your team being able to deliver results in the form of products or services that are **better, faster, cheaper and easier**. The marketplace will immediately use such products or services.

In recent business history, "WhatsApp" and "Uber" are two big solutions which served this principle, and reaped its benefits. Uber has a solution and claims to be the largest taxi service in the world without owning even a single taxi. Similarly, WhatsApp is today's most commonly used social messaging system across the world. There are manufacturing companies like TATA Motors, Bosch, Samsung and Tesla that have proved this principle to be true and created an impact at the marketplace.

Let us understand the mono and metro trains that run in different metros of the world today. They give the passengers a better experience by helping them commute faster; they are better than aeroplanes where, for a flight of 60 minutes, you wait 3 hours at the airport; and they are accessible, which means they are easy to use for the customer. Secondly, their anti-braking system created by Bosch Technologies also serves the same principle.

Let us look at some websites: Amazon, Gmail and Alibaba have applied the same principle.

Let us look at some products: The Tata Swach water filter without electricity, and the entire pen industry have undergone a change due to this principle.

It is important to learn that these companies built these services and products due to their inside-out approach towards business. All of them focused on the strengths they had and then worked on the above principle to solve a problem at the marketplace.

> *You always have to solve a problem at the marketplace. The more common the problem, the better and faster is the scale of business.*
>
> *– Yogesh Pawar*

If you want to create a culture of **better, faster, cheaper and easier** in your organization, your people need to have the relevant skills and behaviors, as they will be creating an impactful organization in the marketplace. Those skills and behaviors are very different from the skills and behaviors required to build an efficient organization. **Based on the vision of the leader, and the maturity cycle of the organization, a strategic decision of Efficiency or Impact needs to be taken for the success of the organization.** For example, building a reporting system that will make people more disciplined, is an **Efficiency** parameter. However, an acquisition or merger of a business that will elevate or decrease the scale of business, is an **Impact** parameter.

Below are listed skills or behaviors that successful leaders identify, segregate and align with the perspective of the marketplace and the competencies of their people to create a culture of **better, faster, cheaper and easier** in the organization.

In the space given below, list down the names of the relevant people in your organization (or if they are still not on your team, make a list of potential team members) who display these skills or behaviors.

- Identify, segregate and align creative people.

____

____

____

- Identify, segregate and align innovative people and their ideas.

____

____

____

- Identify, segregate and align people who have the ability to strategize.

____

____

____

- Identify, segregate and align people who look at the bigger picture.

____

____

____

- Identify, segregate and align people who proactively engage at the workplace.

____

____

____

- Identify, segregate and align people who have the ability to communicate.

____

____

____

If you notice, people become the central theme of creating an impactful organization – an organization that creates an impact of great value in the marketplace. However, there is an important observation I wish to draw your attention to. What we expect our people to do in the organization sometimes contradicts the behaviors required to create an impactful organization.

Example 1: Innovation is a strong, impactful activity that will create an impact in the marketplace. But, innovation can also fail, and on the other hand, we also need employees to be efficient and do repetitive tasks. Hence, cultural mismatch and confusion start building in the organization.

Example 2: The Ability to be Effective at the Strategic Level as well as the Operational Level – You need to have two different skill sets to achieve strategic and operational objectives. But many times, strategic objectives are put on the back burner and the focus is only on day-to-day operations.

A million-dollar question arises in today's dynamic business scenario – how do you, as a leader, balance both – the repetitive and impactful tasks?

This is where your vision and core values play the most crucial roles. Create them strongly and sincerely with a lot of attention, because defining them is a scientific process of defining where you want to go as an organization and why.

Your ability to balance the repetitive and impactful tasks will create strong value in the marketplace.

Refer to the **Balanced Score Card** method of aligning your people. It is a tool that will help you create both types of communication up to a great level. (Scan the QR code given in Chapter 2 to watch my video explaining the Balanced Score Card.)

Every individual in the organization needs to know where he is going, which means leaders in the organization need to be clear about their personal vision and align it to the organization's vision. Aligning their individual values with the organization's values will allow them to be persistent in difficult times during their success journey. Based on the two vital ingredients – vision and values, you will be ready to work out your organization's strategy to create an impact in the market.

Let us have an understanding of what you should focus on when you create the indicators of vision and values. Successful leaders understand this. They proactively create systems that allow the organization to be built on core values and a well-defined purpose.

For example, if you are on the first gear while you drive the vehicle on a highway and on top gear when you are in traffic, accidents are inevitable. While it is easy to shift gears and control a car, it becomes difficult to quickly change gears in an organization due to dynamic human behavior. People with different beliefs, values, cultures, and most importantly, motivations, come together to fulfill their dreams and aspirations in an organization. Your products and services are the modes through which they can achieve them.

Successful leaders create a safe boundary for all employees and thus, give them a ground to play. Due to this process, employees definitely know what they should do versus what they shouldn't. Successful leaders invest their time in developing these guidelines and create a system for employees to follow and for themselves to monitor. They provide the vision to the company and challenge the intelligent minds of people to perform to their fullest. They guide them through their successes, and most importantly, empower them to take risks and achieve results that create an impact in the market.

Apart from people, successful leaders invest time in future decisions based on data; this is called business prediction. Many times, leaders make decisions because they are able to observe the patterns in the data, which are reflected from the market; they have no prototype to prove it, but as mentioned earlier, they draw logical conclusions and stand by them.

Ask yourself – What do you really feel about the next big change in your industry, and can you logically prove your company's leadership in the marketplace by foreseeing and implementing it?"

If you are not yet sure, then create a plan and a picture of how you can create a logical sequence to let the market understand that the product or service that you intend to bring to it is relevant to help customers become **better, faster, experience ease and most importantly, have the product/service cheaper than in the past.** Authors of *Blue Ocean Strategy*, W. Chan Kim and Renée Mauborgne, say, **"Value Innovation occurs only when companies align innovation with utility, price and cost positions."**

How do leaders behave at the marketplace to create Value Innovation?

1. By creating products/services that are BETTER, FASTER, CHEAPER and EASIER – the market calls this Value Innovation
2. By facing challenges and opportunities courageously and intelligently
3. By perceiving change as a creative process
4. By believing in delayed gratification – humility, gratitude and giving
5. By talking about their Vision, Mission, Values and Impact tirelessly

Let us understand these points in detail.

1. **Creating products/services that are BETTER, FASTER, CHEAPER, and EASIER – the market calls this Value Innovation**

As a leader, you must build your strategy such that you are able to fulfill the principle of BETTER, FASTER, CHEAPER, and EASIER. Every time you are able to do that, you are on the path of creating an organization that is impactful and growing with sustainable profits. Mind you, this is a continuous process. On a lighter note, I have heard that to keep the romance alive in your love or marriage, you need to do something different every seven years. When it comes to business, this time period is less than three years. Build your long-term goal, but every three years, you must change your strategies and map your successes and failures with your big goal. The third year has to be a leap towards a change.

Does this mean that you have to wait for three years in order to change? The answer is no.

Successful leaders proactively approach change and make it happen; their ability to create impact is the key to their success.

2. **Facing challenges and opportunities courageously and intelligently**

A strong "Niti" (the Sanskrit term for Strategy), written by the great philosopher and king's counsellor, Chanakya, is as follows, **"As soon as the fear approaches near, attack and destroy it."** It was 375-283 BCE when Chanakya said this; however, in business scenarios, it still holds true. Any change generates some fear in you or any individual. The degree of fear will change with the impact of the change that you perceive. For example, if you lose your wallet while walking down the street, you will be worried for an hour, a day or a week. However, if you lose your job, have a family to take care of, and are the only breadwinner, the fear is far more. However, over the years, great leaders build a very strong attitude of fearlessness. Hence, they face market challenges and opportunities courageously and intelligently. This one quality has taken leaders from good to great, because the bigger the positive change they can accomplish due to their fearlessness, the more successful they are as leaders.

Say, *"IT'S OKAY,"* move on and do what you are supposed to do, and not what you are comfortable doing.

— Yogesh Pawar

3. Perceiving Change as a Creative Process

In my observation, great leaders have always created something that created an impact; they are so busy in creation that they have no time to fear.

Remember, creation is on the **Impact** side of the graph, as shared earlier. Leaders create suitable products, services and solutions, and face the change to make profits and to create an impact in the market.

4. Believing in Delayed Gratification – Humility, Gratitude and Giving

As change catalysts, great leaders are aware of the importance of delayed gratification at every moment of their lives. They imbibe this principle within themselves and create a logical pattern to explain it to the world around them (at times to the society or the company or to any marketplace). They are aware that if they succeed, they will be appreciated in the end, but during the journey, they will be blamed, taunted and looked down upon. But, in spite of this, their beliefs, values and vision keep them going. This ability to embrace delayed gratification makes them successful. There are a lot of failures as well as unsuccessful moments that they face but due to a clear vision, a courageous heart, delayed gratification and persistent actions, they reach their desired goals. When you are in a leadership role, there will be turns, speed breakers and potholes but if you have decided on your goal, it is better to start enjoying the journey.

5. Talking about their Vision, Mission, Values and Impact tirelessly

Leaders talk about their vision, mission, values and impact to employees, family, friends, investors, bankers, and stakeholders, and also speak about these everywhere. They create enough visual and emotional triggers for the people around them and ensure that everyone around them too starts believing in their vision, mission, values and impact.

There are two reasons behind doing this. Internally, they need feedback during the process, and secondly, they make people aware of their vision, mission, values and impact.

Let us do an exercise to understand the science behind why leaders need to talk about their vision, mission, values and impact to people tirelessly. Ask your teams or family the following two questions.

> Who is the king of the jungle?
> Instruct your team members to point their finger towards where they feel the North Star is located.

To which question did you get the correct answer and why?

Where the North Star is located, is definitely less known as compared to who the king of the jungle is. Why? This is because you don't see the North Star commonly on your television channels, nor is it spoken about often. But, when it comes to the king of the jungle, all our fairy tales have long established that the lion is the king of the jungle. Our parents taught us, we read about it ourselves, sketched lions, saw them in the circus, and on TV shows, and understood the reason behind them being called the kings of the jungle.

The same information repeated over a period of time in various forms, creates a belief system.

Now, we know that whether it is a jungle in Africa or India or the Amazon, a lion is a lion, and he is the king of the jungle. It is like the Law of Gravity. It is the same in New York City, in China, and in Somalia, and everywhere around the world. Why do you think you believe that the lion is the king of the jungle? Simple, because this information has been continuously repeated to you in various forms, and is still being repeated. This is what great leaders master; they keep talking about their vision, mission, values, goals and impact until these become a part of the organizational DNA.

Individuals in an organization can have different personal goals, but organizational goals need to take precedence over any personal goals. People need to set aside personal goals and work together to achieve the common goals of the organization. It is the leader's job to get people to work towards common goals.

– Yogesh Pawar

If all the employees and leaders in your organization look in the same direction, you are in a great state, where you can not only scale up your business but also live a successful entrepreneur's life. But, if all of them look in different directions, then there is the challenge of the company not growing, high attrition levels, disengaged people, and lack of ownership. Your ability as a leader is being questioned when people in your organization do not know the direction or the top agenda of the company and the reason behind it.

Do not get tired and blame people if they don't accept change. Speak to them tirelessly. Remember, continuous information given in different forms creates a belief. Follow the two stages of disseminating the vision, mission, values, goals and impact:

Stage 1: Who are the positive influencers in your organization? (They need not be your direct reportees. These influencers can be anywhere in the organizational pyramid.)

Stage 2: Get these people together on a regular basis (I recommend monthly), and start teaching/training them in what you believe. In 90 days, that is, in three months, you will realize two things.

1. Are they your real positive influencers or was that your own perception? The signal is simple. If they are not your real positive influencers, they will listen to you but their actions will not be the minimum required ones.
2. Your real positive influencers will give you a sign of acceptance. This means that your vision has started percolating into them. This is the time when you start encouraging them to build systems for the future.

Keep doing this activity until these positive influencers start believing in the change.

Personal Effective Behaviors of Great Change Leaders

There are personal effective behaviors that great change leaders display in the process of change for creating an impact.

1. Give and Share What You Know

Sharing comes from the deep-rooted philosophy of interdependence on each other as humans. In the course of our life, we are dependent on each other for the smallest things. Then, we become independent and form our own beliefs and values to live our lives, and lastly, we become interdependent on the ecosystem that we create.

Successful leaders understand and follow this philosophy of interdependence, and quickly become mentors to people around them. They realize that it is important to share their intellect and wisdom with the people around them so that they become better at what they are doing.

Hence, make it a habit of sharing what you know. Only then will your team and subordinates perform better. Your job as a successful leader is to give what you know so you can acquire new knowledge and skills to perform bigger and better tasks. This one people habit will make you hungry for doing more for yourself and the people around you.

2. Handle Your People's Failures Intelligently

The later chapters describe how you can handle the failure of your team members and subordinates. Your people's behavior demands that you be tolerant of the mistakes they make. Failure makes them wiser. Hence, their ability to take risks will increase. You would have gone through the same stage when you were at that position.

3. Encourage People to Do More

Encourage people to take risks, work as a team, face new challenges and also be passionate about their work. The best way to encourage people is to behave the way you want them to. Give them responsibilities and trust them. Encourage them and motivate them to do more. While helping people grow, you are assisting them to achieve their personal vision due to which, your people become committed to the organization's vision, because individual excellence will lead to organizational excellence.

4. Always Let Them Ask Questions When in Doubt

Let your people ask you questions. Why should something be done? What should be done? Who should do it? When should it be done? Their questions will depend upon their stage of maturity in their job roles. You too, as a leader, need to question people about their ideas. It helps them to think and rethink achieve the desired results.

5. Give Credit to the Team

The mantra to create a long-lasting performing team is, "Failures are the leader's responsibility, while success belongs to the team." Never miss giving credit for the contribution that people have made and the role that they have played in the team's success. Make sure you find opportunities to give your people credit for all the good things that they do.

A question here is, why don't leaders praise their people often? This is because such leaders are in doubt about themselves and about their team accomplishing the task.

To overcome this, make sure that you are hundred percent clear about what you want your people to deliver, and then, just trust them to do it. Encourage the smallest achievement and give credit for everything that they do to impact the market positively.

6. Know your People's Limitations, and Accept them Wholeheartedly

One of the most important people behaviors of successful leaders is knowing how competent and future-ready their teams are. So, do you know your team's competencies and whether they are future-ready? There could be a skill gap, or the orientation given to a team member is not sufficient for him to do a certain task or to lead a certain change. Leaders identify the best squad and cover the weakest link in the team or the weakest ability of the team with their own competencies or by managing performance. They do so by exposing people to better information, better knowledge, better training, better coaching and this is how employee learning becomes an integral process for any change leader.

7. Be Straightforward All the Time and Speak the Truth

The shortest distance between two points is always a straight line. Hence, save yourself time by saying what you want to say rather than what you don't want to say. Successful leaders are always assertive in their communication. They are able to express their emotions, context and actions through every conversation that they have with their employees or colleagues. This is a skill to be learned. Hence, don't waste time experimenting with it. Just do it, learn it and practice it relentlessly. Be an assertive human being, and speak the truth about any situation that you go through, or that you are expecting to go through.

8. Maintain Good Relationships and Friendships

There is always a personal relationship that can take over any professional relationship. Over a period of time, when people work together, they become good friends. Be great professional friends and always maintain a relationship that can benefit you personally and professionally. When an employee parts from you, always make sure that there is a smooth exit. Let the person leave your company or your leadership with good memories. Believe in the karmic cycle – what goes out, comes back again. Hence, good relationships will always yield great results for your future as a leader.

9. Be a Good Diplomat

Learn diplomacy, learn to balance yourself, stay neutral, and most importantly, be firm about the vision of the company. There are people in the organization who can suck your energy and distract you from your vision. Hence, stay away from gossiping or badmouthing your subordinates, colleagues, or even top leaders. Taking a diplomatic stance helps you question the mediocre behavior in the company. This personal behavior will help you gain respect among your people and their belief in you strengthens.

10. Don't Intimidate Others. Celebrate Small Successes.

I remember the line from the "Spider-Man" comic book which goes, "With great power comes great responsibility." When you take up a leadership role, you are serving people and a bigger cause. Be humble during this process. There are leaders who intimidate others with their position. Make sure you aren't one of them.

Also, an important behavior of successful leaders is that they celebrate every aspect of their work. Not only do they celebrate successes, but they also celebrate failures as stepping stones to learning. Small celebrations effectively create positive energy in the team. Successful leaders find reasons to celebrate. They don't just wait for big successes, they also focus on the small successes that people achieve, and make them accountable for the big ones. A leader could have a celebration to recognize someone on the team, acknowledge the team's efforts even if they failed, welcome a new employee, or bid farewell to an old one.

> *Transmit your positive energy to people through these celebrations. Find a way to get them together and keep them together.*
>
> *— Yogesh Pawar*

To Summarize:

> When an impact has to be created at the marketplace, "People" are at the center of your strategy.

> Create a culture of **better, faster, cheaper and easier** in your organization.

Better – products and services than what you delivered

Faster – than your earlier processes as well as the competition

Cheaper – for your customers

Easier – for your employees and customers to understand and implement

> Never have contradictory values in the organization. Create strong guidelines, and give your people the freedom to operate within those guidelines.

> Your strategies of creating an impactful organization must focus on:

People, Customers, Employees, Finances, and the Market. However, the priority of what comes first depends on the vision you have as a leader.

NOTES:
Your interpretation of this chapter:

Learnings that you will implement:

CHAPTER 4

ACHIEVING SUCCESS THROUGH PEOPLE

> *People coming together with a common cause and moving forward in the same direction create profits at the marketplace. If not, losses are certain.*
>
> *– Yogesh Pawar*

This chapter begins with the analogy of driving from Point A to Point B.

Let us understand what successful leaders do and how they explore success through people. Assume that you are the driver of a car, and that your car can accommodate only three more people.

Because you are the owner and driver of the car, you have the authority to choose the passengers. You are travelling from Point A to Point B, and it requires four hours. There are three milestones that you need to cross. We will call them Milestone 1, Milestone 2 and Milestone 3.

Before you begin your journey from Point A, you meet your friends. One is going in the direction that you are going, till Milestone 1, the second one is going till Milestone 2, and the third is going in the opposite direction. Which friend/friends would you give a lift to?

Obviously, the first and the second friends. You would be okay to drop the first friend at his destination of Milestone 1, and the second friend at Milestone 2, even though they may not accompany you all the way to Point B. But you wouldn't give the third friend a lift, as he is going in the opposite direction.

This means that you will only give a lift to the people who are going in the same direction as you are. You wouldn't take along someone just because you know him or her, or because he or she is a good human being, or because you like the person. These factors are, no doubt, considered much later as part of the decision-making process. However, the first question that enters your conscious mind is – "IS THE PERSON GOING IN YOUR DIRECTION?"

Your vision for the organization is showing you the direction that you have to take. Just as you don't give a lift to people who are not going in your direction, why should you hire people who are not in line with your organization's vision?

Just because they are competent or skilled, or you have a good relationship with them, does not justify your hiring that person. The first question you need to ask yourself as a leader is – does the person share the same or similar value system that you have, and is the person the right cultural fit? It is only after answering this question that, his/her skills, competencies and behaviors need to be checked.

> *Avoid hiring people who don't belong to a similar value system as that which you intend to drive in the organization. Successful leaders only choose people who want to go in the same direction as them.*
>
> *– Yogesh Pawar*

Remember, you and your team will enjoy the journey if you are moving in the same direction. Let us now apply this analogy to the current setup of our organization.

Assume that your organization is your car. You, the leader or owner, are its driver and have the controls. Which people to hire in your organization is your choice.

Ask yourself – Do I hire people keeping in mind the objectivity of the goals to be achieved in that particular year, or do I hire people during knee-jerk emergencies? If you don't undertake manpower planning for the entire year, which is a part of your Annual Operating Plan, you will fall into the trap of knee-jerk hiring and that is definitely a big hurdle in achieving success through people and scaling up your organization. Successful leaders know exactly what kind of people they want in the organization. They focus on the cultural fit, behavior and skills of the individuals they hire. These factors become even more important when they hire for crucial positions in the company.

Hiring plays a major role in creating a robust organization, which builds a legacy in the future. As a leader, you are creating an ecosystem. This ecosystem requires people who lead and people who follow. However, the major challenge is that the leader should identify at what stage the person who is following can lead, and the person who is leading needs more or bigger goals to achieve. This can act as an awesome retention tool. People are always outgrowing their goals/roles and the leader should identify this before they get stagnated.

When I was working with a telecom company, our CEO once said in a conference that he was not the Chief Executive Officer but the Chief Engagement Officer. I always wondered why he said that. After I got into consultation and after coaching leaders for over a decade now, I completely agree with him. As a leader, if you become the Chief Engagement Officer of your people, the magic starts happening.

As a learning habit, I interview a lot of leaders and coaches across the world today. One similar interview was with Dr. Marshal Goldsmith, the world's No. 1 Executive Coach. When I asked him about the biggest challenges that organizations face when it comes to people, he said that there are only two problems:

1. Hiring people – When you hire a wrong person, he will always have performance issues due to not fitting into the role.
2. Managing them – If you hire the right person and are not able to manage him well, not able to craft a journey for him, not able to share your vision with him, not able to give him ample tools to perform and ignite his creative freedom, you will always have a performance challenge.

Let us understand a little about hiring, by focusing on the behavior and approaches you must have to hire people. Assume that you are hiring someone in your company.

Ask yourself these questions and answer "yes," "no" or "maybe."

- Do I know my organization's culture? Yes/No/Maybe
- Do I have the requisite talent to identify talent? Yes/No/Maybe
- Did I plan this resource hiring during my yearly revenue plan? Yes/No/Maybe
- Do I know the top five specific tasks that the resource should perform? Yes/No/Maybe
- Do I know the top five specific behaviors that the resource should exhibit? Yes/No/Maybe
- Do I know the top five skills that I am ready to invest in for the resource to develop? Yes/No/Maybe
- Do I know the top five behaviors that I/the organization has zero tolerance for? Yes/No/Maybe
- Do I have a Plan B if the resource doesn't perform? Yes/No/Maybe
- Do I have a resource available in the current structure that can be optimized? Yes/No/Maybe

- Am I ready to wait for a resource until I find the best match? Yes/No/Maybe

If the answer to most of these question is "no" or "maybe," then it is time to invest in yourself. Successful leaders answer "yes" to all these questions. The key point to realize is, leaders who fail to identify talent, fail in creating great organizations because only when the right people come together and work towards a common goal or a vision are great organizations born.

Identify the right talent and get your organization on the path of greatness. Your products and services may be great, but finally, it is your people who can make or break the company.

Let us understand how a leader should identify the right talent outside or new hires internally. The internal radar of a leader or entrepreneur works in a certain format while making a decision. As leaders and entrepreneurs, we often make mistakes while identifying the right human resources. In common terminology, it is called an "Expectation Mismatch." This causes various issues when you handle people and their emotions at the workplace. If we have a methodology to understand these traits that is simple, our decision-making process will become faster and, hence, I have worked towards identifying categories of behaviors that people display while they perform their day-to-day tasks.

Disclaimer: The following is an analogy for readers to remember and identify behaviors through the Association Thinking Method. I have used the examples of five animals and their behavioral traits. I apologize to readers who may be offended by the analogy. However, nowhere do I intend to frame, demean, insult, judge or stereotype human beings. They all have the ability to be groomed to higher levels. I also do not in any way intend to insult, demean, or judge animals. All animals are precious and without them, life as we know it would be incomplete.

The Five Types of Animals in the Organization Jungle

1. **The Donkeys**: The ones who need constant support for any action.

Fig. 9 The Donkeys

The following are the top seven traits that these people display during their day-to-day behaviors:

- They need to be told what to do every day.
- They don't start by themselves.
- They don't know why they are working.
- They have small goals.
- They are very happy when the work is finished.
- They have a fixed personal agenda in the evening.

What this means is that these people are risk-averse. They constantly worry about things that might go wrong. Hence, they either delay decisions, or constantly need support to make them. The worst part can be that they may work at any level in the organization. Just imagine having them at one of the crucial positions! They have to be pushed through change, and they take time to accept anything new. Most of the time, in order to get them going, the leader needs to use his authority (Instructive Management Style) and not rely on his influence to get the job done. However, once they do the job, they have the unique ability of doing the same task repeatedly. As per my observation, they don't have big dreams, and they often lack focus or a sense of purpose.

These people display a great trend of loyalty towards the person that they work for or their immediate manager, and they are ready to get into unknowns if that person motivates them to do so. They are often very happy and satisfied with the life they live. Generally, they have opinions about how life should be lived and also enough excuses about why they are not able to live that way. My observation is that they have a very good social circle, which they enjoy, and they generally plan almost daily to be with that group of people.

As a leader, how will you handle and develop them?

To handle such people effectively, make sure that

- You have set the right expectations.
- They have a written job description to operate on.
- You stay connected to them through various means.
- You help them understand the purpose of being with the organization on a continuous basis.
- You connect the positive/negative impact of their work on the overall performance of the organization and repeat it at intervals.
- You constantly tell them how they can add value to the department they work in.

2. **The Intelligent Donkeys:** The ones who know what to do, but need to be told to take action.

Fig. 10 The Intelligent Donkeys

The top trends they display during their day-to-day behaviors are:

- They know what to do but need to be told to take action.
- They are diligent in their work.
- They don't know what's happening around them.
- They frequently get tired.
- They are honest.
- They are experts at their jobs.
- They work from 9 am to 6 pm.

These are individuals who know exactly what has to be done, but often, they require an external trigger to get them going. They are dedicated to the work and the task assigned to them. However, that task needs to be given to them, as mentioned earlier. They have no clue, or maybe, they know very little about what is happening in the company, department or even the industry. They are more aligned to their given task and concentrate on completing it. Basically, they are too occupied in their own world to research or to be more creative or innovate in their processes. Being very diligent in their work makes them dependable to get a certain task done. Because of this, leaders don't experiment in assigning them tasks outside their comfort zones and hence, their true potential is never utilized.

The time required for them to adjust to a changing situation or process is high. But they do have the amazing ability to work towards a process that is well-defined with minimal deviation. They generally get uncomfortable with changes that happen dynamically. People with these traits are also disciplined in adhering to their deadlines. All of these traits make them individuals that are dependable but reluctant to change.

As a leader, how will you handle and develop them?

- Ensure that these people have key performance indicators clearly drafted for them.
- Induce change very slowly and with their complete consensus.
- Once they do a certain task a number of times, leave them to do their work with the least interference.
- Most of the time, they just need your affirmation. Stop yourself from giving them your own learnings or experience. Let them make their own decisions about their work.
- Help them to get exposed to various sources of information.
- Proactively add them to cross-functional teams or projects.
- Find opportunities to motivate and appreciate them often.
- Place them in jobs/tasks where there may not be a direct impact but where strong efficiency in performance is required.

3. **The Ponies**: The ones who look like horses but are intelligent donkeys.

Fig. 11 The Ponies

The top trends they display during their day-to-day behaviors are:

- They look like horses, but are intelligent donkeys.
- They have a high self-image.
- They are experts at their jobs.
- They stay with donkeys and intelligent donkeys.
- They need to be motivated at regular intervals.
- They play the role of "jack of all trades."
- They know everything that is happening around them.

This is the breed where most leaders fail. This is the transition state of people where they neither act like horses, nor are they donkeys or intelligent donkeys. However, the ponies feel that they are ready. Now, their own perception about themselves is always better as compared to other people's perceptions about them. In this stage, these people truly believe that they can make a great mark in the organization. They generally overcommit to people and then fail. However, being genuine at whatever they do, they cover up their actions. During the hiring process, they seem to be the most promising candidates. However, they also shoot in the air a lot.

They have a very high self-image, and want to show off their talents to others. They want to be known as smart people. Very often, if these people are given some unknown or challenging task, they shy away and tend to come up with reasons for not doing it. They have spikes in their behaviors, and often need to be motivated by the leader. It is also important that the leader recognizes them in front of other people for their work. They are in close connection with the leader and tend to act in a "jack of all trades" role in the organization.

In a case of this type, scientific methodologies of hiring, like Behavioural Event Interviews, are important and significant to identify the right talent.

As a leader, how will you handle and develop them?

- Connect with them emotionally.
- Manage the task and relationship rationally.
- Let them know that you are watching them.
- Send a clear message that you as a leader are objective in nature.
- Encourage them to take up more tasks. Appreciate and recognize them often.
- Politely inform them that you are not interested in gossip.
- Help them create their personal goals and take a personal interest in following up with them for the same.

4. **The Amazing Horses:** The ones who know that they know.

Fig. 12 The Amazing Horses

The top trends that they display during their day-to-day behaviors are unique and can be noticed immediately.

- They are focused on what they want from the organization.
- Most of the time, they have a high intelligence quotient, due to which, they display their knowledge during any instance where there is a public gathering in the company.
- They know their job well and have a strong mindset of correcting people. Hence, they are perceived as rigid. They are more often closed-door individuals and love to work alone on their terms. It is not that they don't work in teams, but they prefer working alone in silos. When they work in teams, their importance for a project has to be managed by the leader. They are excellence-oriented individuals and want people to notice their work.
- They show supremacy over people due to their knowledge, and although people respect them for their intellect, they may not get along with them.

- Their individual goals are always above organizational goals, and if the time comes to choose between individual and organizational goals, they tend to choose the former. This is not necessarily wrong, but in many instances, the organizational goals are left behind.

As a leader, how will you handle and develop them?

- Give them projects that they can handle individually.
- Ensure that they are recognized at regular intervals.
- Start a coaching program for them. The possibility of them moving up the ladder is higher if they are given a new perspective towards their personal success through organizational goals.
- Work out an individual goal plan with them, and help them achieve it.
- Be ready for surprises that they might leave you halfway in the journey. Till the time they serve the company, they are assets. When they leave, ensure that they leave on a good note.
- Ensure that they have a detailed understanding of their career path (it is not only about a pay rise). Help them understand the vision of the company and the significant role they can play in its growth process. (Before that, you definitely need to have a growth plan.)
- If you do not have a growth plan for them from the beginning, ensure that you create one, or you may lose these resources. The ideal thing is to get them involved in the company's bigger goals and vision.
- Keep them engaged. The more engaged they are, the longer you can retain them.

5.   **The Racing Horses**: The ones who are always ready!

Fig. 13 The Racing Horses

The top trends that they display during their day-to-day behaviors are unique and can be noticed immediately.

Before we start describing these people, ask yourself some questions.

- Have you seen a racing horse running without a goal? Yes/No
- Have you seen a racing horse that doesn't have a jockey? Yes/ No
- Have you seen a racing horse who was a born winner and has never lost? Yes/No

I am sure that the answers to all the above questions will be "No." Let us use this analogy in an organizational context. These individuals show completely different patterns:

- They are extremely focused on organizational goals, and always, I repeat, always, put them first. In this process, they also ensure that they align their personal and social goals to the organizational goals, which makes them more focused on what they do.
- They always use inclusive language that supports the growth of the organization. They are individuals who truly understand the

meaning of ownership and are ready to display it on a consistent basis during their work life or personal life. It is important for them to feel a sense of belonging to the organization that they work with.

- They often get motivated by challenges and achieving greater heights for the organization. Very importantly, they are self-motivated and require bigger and more challenging tasks.
- They are willing to put their heart, brain and mind (emotions, intelligence and stability) into their work when they feel for the organization and believe in the organization and the leader's vision.
- They are optimistic about their career and are confident that they will be able to make a difference wherever they perform. Due to this fundamental orientation and belief system, they tend to perform in almost every organization that they work for. Organizations also actively seek such people and are ready to offer them the best pay scales in the market.
- They view organizational goals as milestones to achieve their personal, professional and social goals.
- They display the need to contribute, and openly share their expertise with whoever is in need of it.
- They are proactive in nature and often work well with teams to produce results.
- One of the strongest abilities that they display is that they have a very strong learning quotient. They operate on a continuous learning mode and have an internal mechanism of experimentation with their own beliefs, skills, and attitudes, and, hence, they creatively find solutions to challenges that the organization faces. This is the most unique skill among all the five types.

As a leader, how will you handle and develop them?

- Make sure they are treated with respect, dignity, openness and given enough protection if they ever fail.
- Make sure they are not compared to anyone else in the organization.

- Coach them on a regular basis with a specific goal in mind.
- Let them know that they are a strong and important pillar of the organization.
- Keep exposing them to new challenges and business goals where they can display their talent and help the organization grow.
- Make them the change leaders of the organization.
- Make them a part of your core decision-making teams.
- Help them explore their personal talent in the process of organizational growth.

To summarize, these five kinds of animals always exist in the jungle called "The Organization." Your ability to identify them, work with them and help them make their way up the ladder is key to your success as a leader. Remember, every animal is required in the jungle to create a balanced ecosystem.

Caution: Due to preconceived notions about how people should be, please do not tag people based on your perceptions and assumptions. Be completely open-minded to learn the various points of view that people bring to the table to solve problems.

Successful leaders understand this universal dilemma of perceptions and assumptions while leading people. Hence, they use the PEARL behaviors (explained in a later chapter) to ensure that they don't leave any element untouched while developing people and achieving the organizational vision.

You, as a leader, need to create a strong ecosystem and the right balance for the animals in the organizational jungle. If you have too many "Donkeys," you will get drained. **It is nothing but self-employment.**

If you have too many "Intelligent Donkeys," you will just be a **supervisor in your own company** or be designated as **Vice President.** But you will still be **a supervisor** caught up in **operational work** rather than being the **strategic leader of the organization.**

If you have too many "Ponies," the **failure ratio** will automatically go up, and **no innovation** will take place. You will be a **drained** and **frustrated leader** with **short goals** like **making money for self-gain or promotions.**

If you have too many "Amazing Horses" and they start working in silos, everyone wants to be noticed and recognized more often as compared to others. You will be a **manager managing people's egos** and **constantly working under the threat of loss of resources.**

If you have too many "Racing Horses," they all want to run, maybe in **different directions.** You will be a leader with **great professional success.** However, you will still **not be satisfied as a human being.**

At every stage, you need to be vigilant about the indicators that your people are giving you and what your actions should be.

We are all products of the environment that we live and operate in. Hence, the kind of environment you create is a choice that you have as a leader. Should it be an environment of autocracy and an environment of diplomacy where rules and regulations are created and twisted as per the leader's wish? Today, in the world where millennials operate and react very fast, it is important for leaders to make decisions dynamically while working with their subordinates. These decisions can only be made quickly and accurately by acquiring one skill: OBSERVATION OF PATTERNS. We are all slaves to patterns that we have created over a period of time. In Chapter 1, we have understood how beliefs and habits are formed. Hence, remember, you have a choice to create a belief system if you are aware of the patterns. If these patterns of people are aligned to the vision of the organization, your success as a leader is definite.

Below is the list of patterns that you may want to observe in your leadership role.

- How often do you inform your people about the vision of the organization?

- Do you often say "yes" when you work with your direct reportees?

- Do you observe the emotions of people when they come to work?

- How often do you discuss and guide your people for living an improved life?

- How do you reward people when they implement developmental feedback?

- What are the learning patterns of the individuals that you observe during their daily operations?

- Do you encourage your team members to learn by themselves or do you handhold them?

- How often do you use the word "I"?

- How often do you conduct dialogues to encourage people to come up with creative ideas?

These are some important attributes that you need to observe about your leadership. In the process, you will be able to gauge your people's capabilities and capacities to drive any change initiatives that lead towards the organization goals.

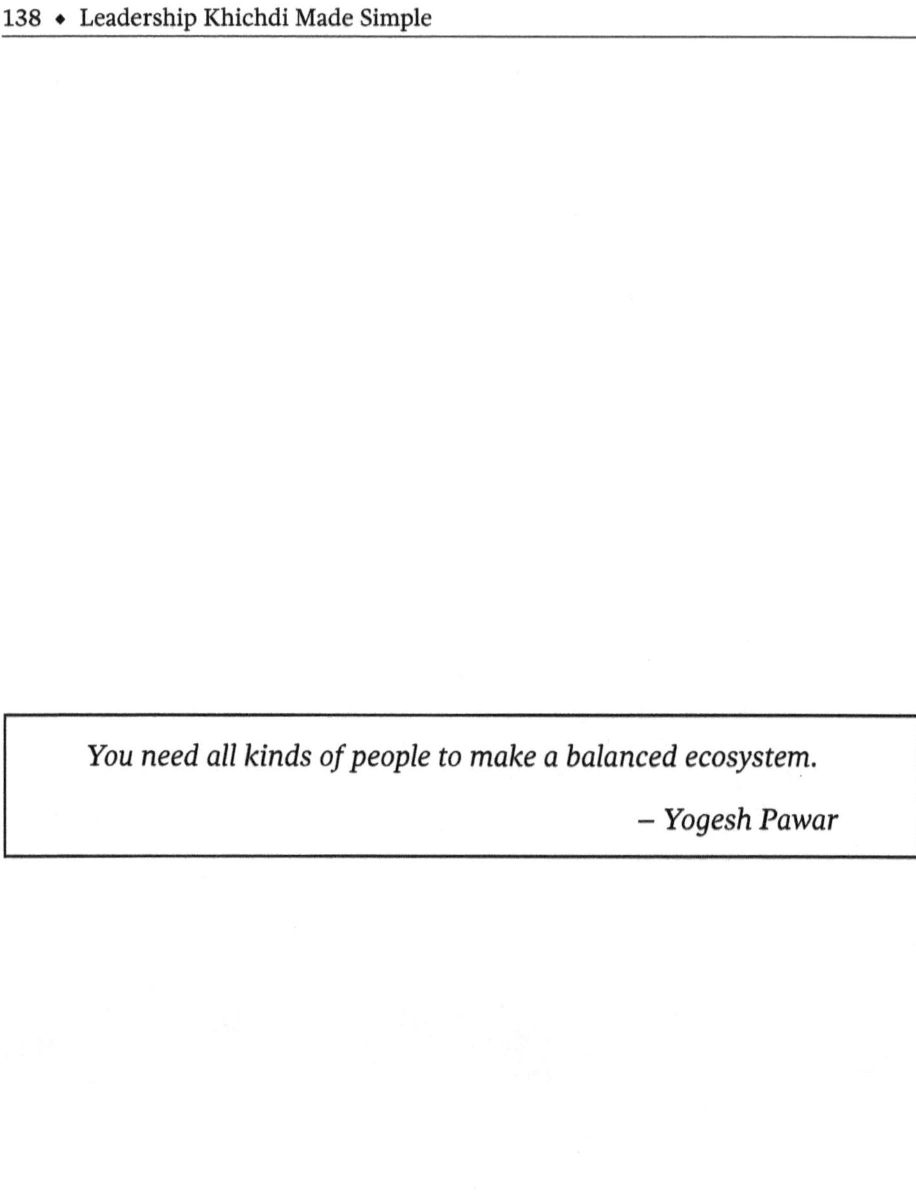

You need all kinds of people to make a balanced ecosystem.

– Yogesh Pawar

The more irreplaceable the skills and behaviors that the person exhibits, the better is the demand for him in the marketplace.

– Yogesh Pawar

Moving Forward

Great leaders treat their people with respect and the utmost trust. They are willing to take business risks through their people.

A great tool that I have found handy for over two decades is the concept of **"Situational Leadership."** I am sharing two classic observations that I have made over the years.

Close Connection

Over a period of time, successful leaders are able to create close connections with people with a like-minded, influential and non-competing attitude who act as counsellors for these leaders. They could be in the form of customers, suppliers, consultants, employees or sometimes, even business competitors. Great leaders create close relations with their people; they are aware of what happens in their lives, personally, professionally and socially. This close connection with their people is the right balance between being human by being empathetic, and being result-oriented.

Support

Successful leaders act as true supporters and are assets for everyone who meets them in their journey of life. They choose how much to help others, but they certainly do. Leaders need to create a giving mindset in order to move forward. This could be the giving of their intellect, expertise, wisdom of any type, or material help in cash or kind. You will find a certain universal magic in giving. Great leaders progress from monitoring people to providing them unconditional support. They are willing to stand by them and make the change happen in the direction of the well-being and growth of the organization.

The more you give, the more you get.

– Yogesh Pawar

Great leaders make the first move. They are only adamant about aspects that are non-negotiable, or have zero tolerance for deviations from the values that they pursue in the organization. The rest, they believe, is manageable. However, leaders who fail to make the first move towards trusting their people often fall into the trap of "Should I?" or even "Why should I?"

Both are self-doubts that don't lead to desired leadership performance. Great leaders have a mindset of "Why not me first?" They take the initiative and start the journey and end up with people who believe in their thought process.

Exercise:

Ask yourself where you stand on a scale of 1 to 10 when it comes to trusting people.

1. I always make the first move when it comes to trusting people.
2. I pardon mistakes as long as they are not causing danger to the organization's values.
3. I support people when they need me.
4. I do what I say and say what I do.
5. I let my people fail and stand by them to support and guide them.
6. I treat people based on their performance and behavior.
7. I take tough decisions whenever required.
8. I love to spend time with my people.
9. I encourage them to learn new things.
10. I always facilitate their journey towards success.

If you scored above 80, you are on the right path.

If you scored between 60 to 80, you are conscious and willing to change for the better.

If you scored below 60, your performance is mediocre. Consistent, conscious and long-term efforts are required if you wish to be in the league of great leaders. Remember, great leaders are willing to trust their people unless they prove them wrong. They support and help them grow as individuals.

> *Trust is a two-way street. You have to start first and keep walking.*
>
> *— Yogesh Pawar*

The Top Five Qualities that Help Leaders Explore the Endless Possibilities of Growth and Profitability through People

1. They Support and Help People Grow Individually

A strong observation over years of working with leaders is that there are leaders who support their people objectively, that is, when it comes to organization-related activities. These are leaders who take personal interest in the growth of their people and as an outcome, people show great professional results, making an impact at the marketplace. These leaders leave a long-lasting impression on their people, even if they part from them professionally. People who work under such leadership tend to come back and work with the same leader whenever an opportunity arises. Hence, leaders who take personal interest in supporting and helping their subordinates grow, always create high-performing teams and have low attrition levels. These individuals who perform, show great results while managing difficult situations, conflicts, change, innovation and money, making the leader and themselves valuable at the marketplace. Thus it is important for you as a leader to focus on the personal aspirations of your subordinates that have a direct impact professionally.

Here is where the trust levels between the leaders and the subordinates are very high. They understand each other's language of performance, they understand their roles effectively, and they collaborate faster and work together towards the increased prosperity of the organization.

2. These Leaders Make the Workplace Energetic and Fun for Employees

Excitement and energy are the most important keys to get performance out of humans. Successful leaders have an uncommon excitement about what they do; this excitement is usually seen, heard or noticed when they perform. Whether it is an email, presentation, sales conversation, personal conversation or a discussion at a social gathering, they leave the mark of an excited person.

Apart from being excited, such leaders also direct this excitement and energy to the people around them, making it fun for them as well.

People initially listen to what you say keenly. However, they start taking actions when they see you taking actions consistently towards the vision of the organization. You as a leader must show them what to do – How should their behavior be? What should their language be?

Unfortunately, a lot of leaders focus on teaching and showing off their skills to their people. Great leaders, however, hire people who know what to do (the skill part) and induce the behavior they expect by showing those behaviors regularly.

Note: As I have mentioned earlier, you take care of the small things for your people and they will take care of the big things for the organization.

Persistence in a leader's behavior will make people believe in him. It could be positive or negative.

Follow these five steps to spread excitement in your people through your actions:

- Stay Motivated: Always stay motivated about your vision in front of your people. (No doubt, it is a tough job!) Just as an actor's performance is judged by the box office, similarly, a leader needs to have a Friday show every day.
- Be Disciplined: On time, every time. Time is not about task management; it is also about your focus and completion of the task as planned. Hence, make it your focus to be on time. There are many leaders who have time issues and make people wait. Remember, people learn from what you do. If you are late, then they will be late too. The worst part is, when they lead, they

will pass on the same thing to their team members. Start every discussion on time and attempt to complete it on time.

- Use humor to connect: When we laugh, we release endorphins (a group of hormones) that make us feel happier and less stressed. When endorphins increase, the stress hormone (cortisol) is reduced. A good laugh can be an effective way to release stressful emotions. Happier employees perform better. Great leaders always have an active funny bone. They make sure that they use humor to connect with people. They create a fine balance between being funny and being comedians. The after-effect of this action is that as a leader, you will always be wanted. People perceive you as approachable, which is a sign of being a great leader. For you to be approachable, you have to be trustworthy. Humor is a good beginning, if it is supported by business actions.

- Be the Reason behind your People's Smiles: A smile on your employee's face can enhance the way he feels, and can make a drastic change in performance. Great leaders have this as a top business priority. As they focus on profits, products and processes, they also focus strongly on people. They realize that people are the real assets, and if they are happy, everything else will follow. You must cultivate the skill of having deep connections with your core team members – those members who really drive the agenda of the organization. Learn the science of making people laugh and making them happy. They will not work for money, but will work for you, putting in their blood, sweat and tears to achieve the organization's goals.

- Support People Unconditionally: When people fail, support them in all the creativity and innovation that they are a part of. People will fail. Due to time and financial pressures, you may lose your temper or tolerance during such times. But, holding that pressure to yourself and supporting them to create action plans in the direction that the organization wants to go is an art. Never knock people down before they try. Even if you know they will fail, let them take the experience.

Caution: However, in such a situation, safeguard the organization from any fatal error.

Your people will learn from you and respect you for supporting them. Always give them "Air Cover Protection" (an analogy used in the military to support your ground army through air force). As long as the error is operational, and not an ethical mistake or a governance issue, a leader should be tolerant.

Let people have their own experiences and let them fail intelligently.

– Yogesh Pawar

3. Great Leaders are interested in their People Personally

People work and perform for their own reasons. Irrespective of how big your company is, the organization's vision needs to be compelling and relatable to the employees' professional and personal goals. Great leaders understand this fact. They ensure that they find the correct reasons for employees to perform. People get motivated only if they feel that they can get something for themselves. It could be a personal, social, family or professional reason. If you as a leader are able to trigger the right chord, you will find your employees highly motivated. Let us understand the reasons that motivate people to perform.

People perform to earn money and spend it on things that are important to them. Great leaders understand why their people earn money and what they spend it on. This is important to know because people spend most of their hard-earned money on what they enjoy/need the most. Understanding the triggers of human behavior will help you gain more for your people and, of course, the organization that you serve.

People perform to either gain pleasure or avoid pain. Great leaders understand this and act accordingly, because everyone gets pleasure through different things, and everyone avoids different kinds of pain.

> *Humans are driven by emotions; every decision or motive behind the action is emotional by nature.*
>
> *— Yogesh Pawar*

4. Great Leaders Help People Constantly Visualize Change

We have understood how personal and organizational rituals are created. This aspect of great leaders is about being creative in the entire change process. The Beyond Conscious Competence Model described in Chapter 1 will help you, the leader, to create a mechanism that will act as a key catalyst to help you visualize the change and also show it to your people.

One of the greatest case studies is that of General Electric when Jack Welch was at its helm. In his book, *Jack Welch and The 4E's of Leadership: How to Put GE's Leadership Formula to Work in Your Organization*, author Jeffrey A. Krames mentions the relentless efforts that a leader has to put in to help people *visualize the change*. Remember, people will not change unless they are able to visualize a better tomorrow and the fun they will have when they change. Unless a pictorial representation is created, they will not be able to see that different company or different department. As they get involved in the journey, only that picture, which is repeated in various forms will keep them going. One very important aspect when you intend to make people change is letting them know that they are progressing. If they don't visualize or feel that they are making headway, they will stop moving forward toward the desired change, and be less persistent about it. This may also lead to employees being disheartened and not adopting the change at all.

During the change process, it is important for the leader to let his people think, feel, act out the change and enjoy the journey. There are various methods to achieve this with the help of the human resources and marketing teams. But, the personal leadership trait to be followed is "Practice what you preach."

5. Leaders Tirelessly Communicate their Beliefs

When I say this, it means that they overcome both physical and mental tiredness. Great leaders constantly communicate the reasons behind, the methods and the expected results of the change that people will go through. During my consultation with business founders and leaders, I have observed a hurdle-creating "wait and watch" approach (procrastination or delayed decision-making) that leaves the people in the organization with ambiguity and doubts. Founders and leaders who have been able to take the proactive approach of consistent communication, have been able to convince people about their vision of the future.

If ambiguity is the roadblock, actions are bound to slow down. Realizing this, great leaders create a safety zone for people who go through change. They are courageous enough to take the blame if change initiatives don't deliver the expected results. During any communication, they clearly state what they want, how they want it and why they want it. The magic is that when they communicate, they make their change a fun journey and create a story that people would love to be a part of.

Remember, **the needs of the minority are most of the time overpowered by the needs of the majority.** But if the thought or the change is beneficial for the organization, and leaders have hundred percent clarity about it, they create a strategic roadmap to convert the minority thought process into a majority thought process. This is just like when, during the beginning of the journey, a founder or leader is either alone or with a handful of people. Slowly but persistently, they create enough evidence so that the majority starts believing in the bigger vision and starts following the leader's thought process.

Use these pointers when you communicate with anyone around you during all your change initiatives:

- What is the emotional benefit that people will achieve through the change and how would it benefit them personally, which is linked to organizational success?
- How would they work through and mitigate the risk involved?
- What is people's role in the change process?

In every communication, great leaders paint a vivid picture of the journey and success. If your communication has the above elements, the possibility of moving forward in the direction of change is higher. People will fail in taking certain actions during the change process and that is alright, as long as you have the clarity of what is supposed to be achieved. Your role is to be a guide, mentor and facilitator in the entire journey of change. Great leaders have the ability of asking the right questions that extract the right emotions, methods and actions from individuals and groups.

Here are the top ten questions that you should ask your people when you see them failing or not moving in the desired direction. Follow the order of questions, for accurate results.

1. Where do you feel you would reach by taking these actions?
2. What are the specific actions you will take in order to reach there?
3. What are the top three results that you anticipate on taking these actions?
4. How do you wish to take those actions?
5. What would you do when you reach the desired result?
6. What are the other alternatives to reach the same result?
7. Why do you feel that this is the right method to reach the desired result?
8. What would you lose if you don't reach the desired result?
9. Why would people buy your idea?
10. How have you visualized the results?

By asking these focused questions, you will help your people who are failing or are not moving in the right direction to visualize a journey. It will allow them to take specific actions and also enrich their experience of failure by deriving learnings out of it. Most importantly, they will respect you for being a guide and mentor that they would always wish to have in their lives.

To Summarize:

➢ People are with you for their own reasons. They will be with you for their reasons only.

➢ You have the authority and choice to choose your people. BE WISE.

➢ There are only two problems with people: Hiring and Management.

➢ There are five types of animals in the jungle called "The Organization."

➢ Be a catalyst in people's journey of personal success.

➢ Trust is the integral foundation for building an organization with people.

➢ Communicate your beliefs tirelessly.

➢ Help people visualize change constantly.

➢ Be interested in them personally.

NOTES:

Your interpretation of this chapter:

Learnings that you will implement:

CHAPTER 5

MAKING THE JOURNEY ENJOYABLE

> *Should one enjoy the journey or the destination?*
> *Great leaders enjoy both.*
>
> *– Yogesh Pawar*

The famous football player Maradona was once asked how he felt when his team Argentina, won the World Cup. His reply was that he felt empty. He explained by saying that the journey of reaching this pinnacle was more exciting to him than winning the World Cup.

This chapter will focus on the three important aspects of the behaviors of great leaders during their journey of achieving their personal or professional goals.

- What are the effective personal behaviors in the process of achieving their goals?
- How do leaders manage failures or setbacks?
- What drives them – the goal or the journey?

Three-Action Behavioral Framework

At the School of Inspirational Leadership, during all our consulting projects, we assist business leaders and entrepreneurs to make their journey enjoyable. The Three-Action Behavioral Framework helps leaders map and execute the journey of reaching their goals more meaningfully and most importantly, more joyfully. This framework becomes the nucleus of the change journey that the business leader operates on. The framework operates on a 3E model: Engagement, Explanation, and Expectation. Let us start with the base of the pyramid – Expectation.

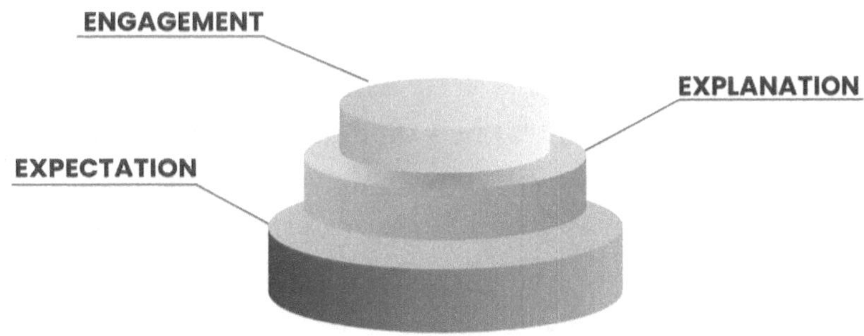

Fig. 14 The Three-Action Behavioral Framework

➢ **Expectation:** Humans are full of expectations. Their expectations might change according to their perception about their environment, knowledge, skills and habits. People work to fulfill their personal desires, using the organization as a vehicle. Hence, in order to achieve success through people, the organization and its people need to have common goals. The only way to achieve this is to set expectations. It is important for leaders to set expectations of performance and behaviors on Day One. There must be a personal dialogue between the leader and the subordinate on a daily basis to ensure that the subordinate understands and comprehends the expectation from his role and the behaviors required to perform/ drive the task. This will leave a long-lasting impression on the subordinates' mind as he starts taking full responsibility for his job and becomes an asset to the organization. This dialogue between a leader and his subordinate needs to be reviewed at regular intervals, because expectations keep changing from both sides. Hence, a proactive dialogue will always assist people to perform better.

Use the following questions while having a dialogue with each of your subordinates:

- What is the vision of the organization and how can he contribute to that vision?
- What will his specific role be during this process?
- Does the existing system ensure that he is made aware of where he is in the journey of reaching the desired organizational goals?
- How often should his performance be reviewed to help him achieve his goals?
- What are the tasks that he would do independently?
- What are the tasks that he would need support for?
- What is the learning he wishes to go through?
- What are the behaviors he needs to display during the process of achieving his goals?
- What does he expect from you, as a leader?
- What does he want to learn from you, as a leader?

Use the following questions when you need to set expectations in a forum with all your subordinates.

- Why does the company exist?
- What are the values of the company and how can everyone align with them?
- What are the top behaviors required to achieve results?
- What are the top five activities that everyone in the organization should focus on?
- How will they display the required behaviors during their daily work?

You can also answer the above questions yourself when you speak to your subordinates in a forum. Your dialogue will inspire your people. It will ensure that they feel that they belong to the organization, and most importantly, help them to stay connected with the bigger cause. Your job as a leader is to continuously pass a message about what you expect, why you expect it and how people would benefit from the expectation and enjoy the journey.

➢ **Explanation:** Humans have a supercomputer called the "Brain," which functions 24x7. Our brain has a unique capacity for storing data. This data gets converted into knowledge and skills only when you apply that data or information. As leaders, focus on what message you want to pass on throughout the organization. Then, keep explaining the message to people tirelessly through various methods. Over a period of time, you will notice that people start responding to your messages, and most importantly, start passing on the same messages. This is an important aspect of a leader's role. In my experience, a few leaders assume that their people have understood the vision, strategy, goals, procedures, processes, rules, etc. This is one of the biggest leadership mistakes. Over a period of time, they meet failure in their journey. It is helpful to pause and regularly give your team members clarity about what is important for the organization, so that they constantly focus on those parameters of success.

Follow the processes given below while explaining your expectations to your subordinates.

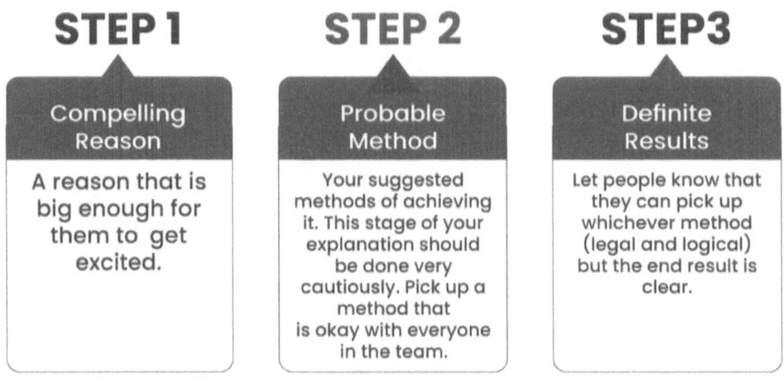

Fig. 15 The Process of Explaining your Expectations

➢ **Engagement:** Organizations are created through people. Any organization is a set of people that operates together with certain belief systems that are created over a period of time. Engaging your employees is the only way to keep them motivated and eager to work every day. An engaged employee performs over 100 percent as compared to an employee who is not motivated. The following is the method that you need to adopt and improve on to have a highly engaged workforce:

- Learn to describe or paint a vivid future for your people.
- Learn to express the complete expectation from each individual and their roles.
- Learn to communicate with them repeatedly, enthusiastically, and with a smile.
- Learn to say no when required.

There are many behaviors that leaders follow in the process of achieving their goals. However, there are three behaviors that stand out in both good leaders and great leaders.

1. Their ability to do a repeated task regularly.

    You will never find leaders getting bored with what they do. They are busy with their work and don't waste a single moment or opportunity to make an impact.

2. They perform only those tasks that they are good at.

    Good and great leaders stay away from personally doing things that they may struggle with. Unless they do things that they are good at, they will not feel successful every day.

3. Every day, they choose only three things that they wish to execute and only work on that agenda.

    This is not a to-do list. This is a personal agenda that makes you feel successful every day. Remember, if you don't feel successful every day, the possibility of you becoming successful is minimum.

Then, who should do the things that you are not comfortable with? That's the logic for finding the right guy for the right job at the right time. Answer these questions, and you will find a quick reference to what you may want to focus on the most in your business.

Exercise:

Rate yourself from 1 to 10 at the following tasks:

1. I love working on new ideas and handing them over for execution.
2. On a daily basis, I love to follow the created protocols.
3. I love to have conversations with people every day.
4. I love to share what I know every day.
5. I love to do challenging tasks every day.
6. I generate ideas almost every day.
7. I sleep peacefully every night.
8. I have a clear agenda every morning.
9. I actively seek information about my work every day.
10. I write long emails to people.

List down the individual tasks where you have scored between

1 to 4	**5 to 7**	**8 to 10**
Eliminate these tasks from your work	Take support from people or set up a system for them to get done	Do only these tasks yourself

Great leaders only focus on the activities on which they scored between 8-10. Hence, their internal feeling is always that of happiness. As a result, people perceive them as leaders who are energetic, passionate, and excited.

With this simple exercise, you will be able to be successful every day. Once you personally start feeling successful as a leader, it will affect three major aspects of your work and your life:

1. Your confidence
2. The ability to say no when required
3. Conviction about any task that you perform

Your people will look up to you as a desired leader – a leader who stands by his words and supports them with the required actions.

This is not rocket science. It is as simple as it is written in this book. The key is your ability to decide what to do and what not to do because at the marketplace, doing what you know is called "experience" and doing what you don't know is called "risk-taking."

Most leaders fail due to the time consumed in executing their vision due to lack of experience, skills and knowledge, which they can easily adopt from teachers, coaches, experts, consultants and advisors. Lack of this awareness creates self-doubt and leads to a fear of decision-making, which delays the entire process of change. Both "experience" and "risk-taking" are choices that are internal by nature and hence, great leaders act based on internal guidelines, which are supported by the advisory council that they create for themselves, through which they improve their decision-making process. Ultimately, both success and failure are consequences of decision-making keeping in perspective the economics and emotions of the change. Great leaders constantly reflect upon their guidelines for decision-making and these guidelines evolve due to the process explained in the model of Beyond Conscious Competence given in Chapter 1. Leadership is about making **the right decision** at **the right place** and **at the right time**. Help yourself and decide what you should and shouldn't do. How this internal guideline is created is explained below.

The truth is that all great leaders depend on the internal radar that constantly guides them. It is displayed to the world around them as their Value System.

The constant behavior you need to adopt as a leader is to map every decision with your internal guidelines – organizational and those of your value system. If it resonates within, then go ahead with the decision. If not, ratify it through facts, figures, opinions and advice from your advisory council and then arrive at the decision's objective.

Great leaders set their internal radar based on the organization's vision, which is guided by a value system. This radar finds all the reasons to create enforcement that suits the decisions that you make. Hence, have a clear, defined personal and organizational vision and value system that guides your decisions along with your trusted advisors and core team. Your vision and value system will be displayed in your actions, your interactions with your stakeholders, processes and systems. Once you are clear with your vision, your rational, intelligent brain gets enough clarity and you can develop the ability that can help you make the right decision. If you don't develop this ability, your decision may go wrong. Leaders having a clear value system and vision often display tolerance towards their people's failures and engage them in getting their decisions right. If their people still fail, leaders do not shy away from being accountable for their failure. Hence, your organizational data, people behaviors, market reports and analyses, and having the right counsel become extremely important during your decision-making process. This is where your organizational data, people behaviors and market facts will bring up various options for you to rationalize the decision that you have taken, or the one you intend to take or deny.

Various stages of organizational growth will require trusted advisors. These are the advisors who you can find and depend on in the course of the organization's growth:

1. Teacher: One who imparts knowledge of a specific subject in a controlled setting.
2. Coach: One who observes and gives you specific inputs that may result in success or failure, but does not get involved in the game with you.
3. Consultant: One who observes you and your business and gives you specific inputs and also gets involved in the game, which may result in success or failure.
4. Advisor: One who looks at the macro perspectives and helps you change the direction of your game.
5. Trusted Advisor: One who looks at the macro perspectives and advises you as your mental counsel.
6. Mental Counsel: A team or a group of people who help you make a unanimous decision. They might be physically present or virtually there with you mentally, and often help you in tough situations of life or business. These could be experts in particular fields whose behaviors you have read about, or have observed closely and you are aware of their positive thought patterns. When faced with a problem related to that expert, you would often wonder, "What would this person do in such a situation?" You get your answer and go on to execute it. For example, if there is a strategic decision to be made to win in the marketplace and if you have read *Nitishastra* by Chanakya and imbibed it, there is a high possibility that your memory would throw back strategies that Chanakya would take in those situations. This would help you to come to a decision.

> *The man who says he can and the man who says he cannot are both correct.*
>
> *– Confucius*

Focus on what You Want Rather than what You Don't

As kids or teens, our internal radar throughout our development is most of the time focused on what should not be done. That is also how we speak to our children. We tell them what not to do rather than telling them what to do.

A simple example is, when our child runs in a park, we instruct him, "Don't run so fast. You will fall," rather than saying, "Run slowly." Our natural belief system starts working on instructions subconsciously and creates a pattern of speaking and understanding based on fear. When the same child becomes a leader, his natural instinct automatically becomes to guide people by instructing them on what not to do rather than what to do.

Great leaders constantly focus on **what has to be done** rather than **what should not be done.** While getting on the path of successful leadership, it is mandatory that you work on forming this habit. Fix your internal radar on what has to be done, and keep it there continuously.

Confidence

The meaning of the word "confidence" is "a feeling or belief that one can have faith in or rely on someone or something."[2]

Confidence is generally described as a state of being certain; either that a hypothesis prediction is correct or that a chosen course of action is the best or more effective.

In both definitions, your **ability to be certain** in a situation and **your ability to display that certainty** make a huge impact on the kind of task or relationship that you are managing as a leader. Let us professionally

---

2   McCumiskey, C. (2018, December 8). *Building confidence requires effort.* Sligo. https://www.independent.ie/regionals/sligochampion/lifestyle/building-confidence-requires-effort-37590667.html. Last accessed on August 03, 2022.

understand what you need to be confident about and where you stand according to your perception.

For this, we have identified skills and behaviors required to move on the path of great leadership. Leaders who have certainty about possessing these attributes display confidence in their actions.

Rate yourself on a scale of 1 to 10 (10 being the highest) on the following attributes that display your confidence to all the stakeholders in your environment.

Attributes	Your Rating
Identifying resources (Identifying the right resources, their requirement in the system, how well they can contribute to the company)	
Public speaking	
Conflict resolution	
Managing ambiguity	
Managing market volatility	
Managing emotional complexities	
Effective writing	
Negotiating and closing deals	
Analyzing data and segregating information	
Creative problem-solving	

If your ratings are mostly above 8, then you have the **ability to be certain** on those specific attributes. However, the **lack of ability to display that certainty** to people or your colleagues might make them perceive you as a submissive leader – a leader who knows a lot of things but fails in displaying them at the right time and the right place.

Self-doubt in a leader delays the decision-making process and leads to continuous ambiguous situations where the people in the organization might feel either left out or confused. In order to improve your certainty about people, situations, system or products, the keyword is

"Repetition." If you repeatedly get into a task, your ability to be certain will increase.

Successful leaders who are already confident and certain, take special care, training and conscious action to **create the ability to display their certainty**. They practice their speeches, plan them well and understand the pulse of the audience and their core needs of why they are with you. They display tolerance in ambiguous situations, manage conflicts with a win-win mindset, and are able to influence people with their thoughts, which help their people move towards achieving the organization's vision.

Activity: Who are the most potential leaders professionally or socially that you have seen/worked with, who have displayed the attributes that are mentioned below?

Attributes	The name of the leader who is your inspiration	An example of how he displayed this attribute	I commit to displaying this attribute during a situation (write down the situation)
Identifying resources (Identifying the right resources, their requirement in the system, how well they can contribute to the company)			
Public speaking			

Attributes	The name of the leader who is your inspiration	An example of how he displayed this attribute	I commit to displaying this attribute during a situation (write down the situation)
Conflict resolution			
Managing ambiguity			
Managing market volatility			
Managing emotional complexities			
Effective writing			
Negotiating and closing deals			
Analyzing data and segregating information			
Creative problem-solving			

When you move ahead on the path of being a great leader, your ability to balance both **your certainty and your ability to display your certainty (meaning your actual skills and the presentation of those skills)** plays an important role in your overall success.

The following is a list of activities that can help to increase your abilities and their presentation, thus impacting your success positively.

1. Read one page a day; anything that is relevant to your work, family or life.
2. Do one activity every day that reinforces your positive belief about yourself.
3. Share your observation personally with at least one person daily.
4. Type or write one page a day.
5. For one minute, close your eyes and visualize your big goal.
6. Help one subordinate or colleague every day.
7. Identify one task that you don't know and that you are ready to learn.

    i. Act on one item daily that improves your business.
    ii. Act on one item that gives you creative freedom.
    iii. Act on one task that you often procrastinate.

The Ability to Say No When Required

Children are experts at persuasion. If they want something, they ensure that they get it. As parents, we give in to them due to love and a lack of patience. We repeat the same mistakes in our companies; when people persuade us, we give in due to a lack of patience or fear.

If you notice, the lack of patience is common in both the scenarios. Chapter 1 talks about creating habits. Refer the figure of the Beyond Conscious Competence Model. Those are also the habits you can create in people through your persistent, rational behaviors.

Just imagine, when your people understand that when a leader says no it means no, what will happen? They understand your certainty. Slowly but with conscious efforts, you will be able to create a behavior pattern of your response. However, as I mentioned, it has to be rational and backed by facts, numbers or data, and not by your subjective beliefs.

Great leaders display this pattern very openly to their people. There are two major benefits of doing so.

- People come to you with action-oriented plans when they are ready.
- Your people are assertive when they are not ready for action/ with plans/goals.

They see you as a leader who is prepared.

What are the personal benefits you achieve through these behaviors?

- You save time.
- You don't get into unnecessary arguments or unproductive actions.

Saying no has great power. When you say no to people based on facts, they either go back and work on their plans/goals to prove their point to you with facts, or they believe in you and your decision of "No."

Caution: Use the ability to say no wisely, as this may cost you in various forms – people, processes, systems or opportunities.

If you cultivate the habit of saying no based on facts and figures, you will be able to save time for what you want to achieve. By using this one phenomenon, you will be able to focus on what is important, which is an integral part of achieving goals.

The Psychology of Pain and Gain

Dealing with pain positively creates character, and great leaders have great personal character. Every human being takes action for only two things:

1. To avoid pain
2. To gain pleasure

However, two more elements are important:

1. Avoidance (the behavior exhibited before the pain)
2. Gain

Pain and pleasure, or avoidance and gain can be extrinsic or intrinsic in nature. If you have envisioned your journey, you can find comfort in your pain.

Successful leaders choose pain or discomfort for themselves as well as others in order to achieve organizational goals. This process of discomfort is called "Change." However, this pain is productive because it is undertaken with the final pleasure in mind – the achievement of organizational goals.

Ultimately, it is the personal choices that leaders make that drive the destiny of those who are following them; in our case, the organization. The choices that leaders make are always rooted in their individual definitions of fear and pleasure.

Both fear and pleasure occur due to "thoughts" and "time." This entire process of experiences is explained in the Beyond Conscious Competence Model. The day the leader is able to maturely understand and does not restrict his thoughts or rationalize them but lets them flow like clean running water, is the time he has utilized his intelligence and created wisdom for himself.

This is when the leader starts accessing his subconscious mind, which has the ability to think big and remain joyous, looks at problems as momentary hurdles and develops the amazing quality of **Persistence**. Through this, visionary leaders are born. A resourceful mind is joyous in nature and hence, a mind away from fear is a mind that has reached greatness in its own sense. In order to walk on this path, observe your thoughts, accept them and often look at yourself as a third person. This will help you become a better leader every day. Never forget, it is "thoughts" and "time" that give us pleasure and pain. As a leader, practice observing your thoughts and time.

To Summarize:

- ➤ This chapter focuses on the three important aspects of the behaviors of great leaders during their journey of achieving their personal or professional goals:

  - Effective personal behaviors in the process of achieving their goals
  - Managing failures or setbacks
  - Understanding what drives them – the goal or the journey

- ➤ The Three-Action Behavioral Framework operates on a 3E model: Engagement, Explanation and Expectation, and helps leaders reach their goals meaningfully and enjoyably.
- ➤ Once you personally start feeling successful as a leader, it will affect three major aspects of your work and your life:

  - Your confidence
  - The ability to say no when required
  - Conviction about any task that you perform

- ➤ Leadership is about making **the right decision** at **the right place** and **at the right time**.
- ➤ All great leaders depend on the internal radar – their Value System. Map every decision with your internal guidelines – organizational and those of your value system.
- ➤ Various stages of organizational growth will require trusted advisors.
- ➤ Great leaders constantly focus on **what has to be done** rather than **what should not be done**.
- ➤ To be a great leader, your ability to balance both **your certainty** and **your ability to display your certainty (meaning your actual skills and the presentation of those skills)** plays an important role in your overall success.

> ➤ If you cultivate the habit of saying no based on facts and figures, you will be able to save time for what you want to achieve.
> ➤ Pain and pleasure, or avoidance and gain can be extrinsic or intrinsic in nature. If you have envisioned your journey, you can find comfort in your pain.

NOTES:
Your interpretation of this chapter:

Learnings that you will implement:

CHAPTER 6

WHAT SUCCESSFUL LEADERS DON'T DO

This is an important chapter of this book. It explains to you what not to do as a great leader. "What not to do" has a relevance beyond an organization and this discipline has to be observed by successful leaders lifelong. If you stay away from these actions, you will get on to the path of being a great leader, which will lead to performance and productivity in whichever marketplace you operate. This chapter consists of methodological ways for you to get away from those habits, which were created over a period of time and were taking you away from the path of being a great leader.

There are five behaviors that a leader should never display and should stay away from:

- Carrying past baggage
- Labeling people
- Losing sight of objectivity
- Allowing rigidity in processes
- Creating an environment of fear

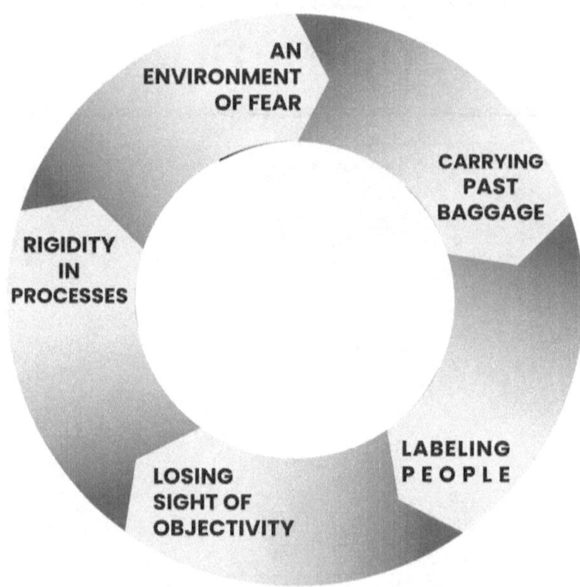

Fig. 16 The Circle of Imbalanced Leadership

The Circle of Imbalanced Leadership

The Circle of Imbalanced Leadership is a downward spiral – the series of behaviors in which the leader may get trapped at any stage of his career. One behavior leads to another and has a ripple effect on the next behavior. Every time the behavior creates instant gratification, the leader tends to repeat it until one day, it becomes a part of him. Through this, a potential leader gets into the trap of these behaviors and thinking patterns, displays them continuously and ultimately, tries to prove that every action of his is correct. When leaders are consciously working towards building teams and businesses, it is important for them to stay away from such actions and behaviors.

➢ **Carrying Past Baggage**

Have you ever failed?

We all have failed at some time or the other. Our failures leave deep scars on our minds and hearts. We hear many stories about people who have succeeded against all odds. We learn and understand the lessons from their stories. However, you will find that not more than 20 percent or even fewer people have really made it big enough for the world to notice. Does that mean that the 80 percent people who fail don't try? No, they do try, but give up most of the time. One of the core obstacles is that 80 percent of the population gives up on what they want due to their own negative baggage of their past failures. These people do start anew but with old thoughts, habits and behaviors, which create a limited belief about people, situations, processes or systems. These limited beliefs are either due to some failures or also major successes in the past about similar people and situations. These 80 percent people who do not make it big do so precisely because of the strong, however, limited belief system that makes them averse to change. During my training and coaching processes, I have noticed that most of the time, they are not even aware that the present failure they are facing is due to their beliefs about the world, which restricts them from taking new actions.

One important behavior noticed in these leaders is that even if they are aware of their behavior they do not accept it in their open environment. They are unaware of the need to change or are resistant to it. **A solution that can pull out leaders from this phase is to openly accept their areas of improvement.** When leaders do this, they drop the negative baggage, which is created based on their past experiences that doesn't allow them to try newer ways of doing things. As a leader perceives that his successes or failures are accepted by his people, and he is accepted as a human, it allows him to relax and become mentally more tolerant. This gives him the mental flexibility to become a leader who is observant about every situation that is ambiguous, uncertain, volatile, or complex during his decision-making process. This also helps him to achieve the basic human need of social acceptance. To understand this phenomenon of human behavior, refer to the Need Theory described in Chapter 7 of this book, based on David McClelland's Theory of Human Motivation.

Carrying negative baggage is the first cause of **Leadership Imbalance.** Leaders get into this trap and start shying away from taking risks and hence, start playing safe. They perform tasks which they know will give them sure success based on their past experiences. This is where a leader becomes less innovative, less creative and less tolerant. This is the beginning of him becoming a selective listener and very selective in trusting people.

This behavior starts repeating, and subconsciously, leaders start displaying mediocre behaviors. This takes them away from the path of great leadership.

The following is an exercise to identify if you are getting into the trap of the **Circle of Imbalanced Leadership.** Observe your language and actions when you interact with people while solving a problem, for the next 21 days.

- Are you expecting new results with your old methods?
- Are you worried that you may lose your position if you fail?

- Are you not able to change a certain behavior in you?
- Do you have difficulty in publicly accepting failure?

If the answers are "Yes," watch out! This means that you may, at any time, become imbalanced and get more involved in the vicious circle of imbalanced leadership.

➢ Labeling People

The second stage of imbalanced leadership is labeling people based on your perception or forming opinions without investigation. This trap, slowly but surely, takes you away from your core business driver, "people." The biggest problem is that this imbalance is driven by **"time"** because as a leader, you feel that time is a scarce resource and you need to take quick, multiple decisions that may impact your personal or professional life. In order to mitigate the risk of failure, a leader labels situations, systems, processes, and especially people, based on patterns.

Additionally, in the process of growing and reaching higher in life, you create experiences that guide your internal focus towards how people should be. Subconsciously, you create mental maps of successful and unsuccessful behaviors. Because your internal focus is limited to specific types of behaviors from people, you tend to expect people to exhibit them. These are a set of positive or negative behaviors that make you subconsciously start labeling people. This categorization that a leader does mentally is called "labeling." Now, in the future, whenever your people perform or don't perform those activities, you have your mental label ready for it.

Most leaders fall into this trap, which is created due to unawareness of a leader's own personal behaviors. We label people when we have any form of interaction with them. This activity that happens subconsciously, makes it easy for us to categorize them and respond to them the next time. The more we do it, the stronger the pattern becomes and the more it becomes a part of our behavior. It is amazing to observe how great leaders consciously stay away from this trap. The solution for not getting into the trap of labeling people is the three steps of understanding the

1.   Intent
2.   Repetition and
3.   Language

in any conversation that you have with people.

Your role as a leader is to understand the **Intent** of the people that you work or interact with. You can understand their beliefs about doing or not doing something through the **Repetitions** that they do. To understand their **Language** means considering the words they use in order to understand their thought process, behaviors and the possible actions they may or may not take. Observant leaders always, I repeat, always, focus on these three aspects when they interact with people. Let us understand all the three aspects in detail.

Intent: It is the motive behind any conversation that you, as a leader, need to focus on. A good leader always concentrates on the core purpose behind the interaction. You may notice that there are people in your team who are not verbal in nature but are good performers. These subordinates feel heard when their leader is able to comprehend the message they are trying to convey. When the subordinates or people that you interact with, realize that their leader understands them, you will start getting results out of every conversation that you have with your people. When you clearly ask the right questions, you understand both the data and the intent, and you will move forward in a direction that will lead the company and you to the desired vision.

A question arises here. Why is it difficult for you to understand the intent of an individual? A very strong observation that I have is that *leaders listen* to their people *selectively* and focus only on *their agenda* in the conversation. Hence, your behavior as a leader also becomes a pattern and this makes it easy for others to manage your response rather than managing the task at hand.

What is the action that you need to take if you wish to understand the intent during any type of conversation? The conversation could be a sales conversation, people issues or even a solution-finding brainstorming session.

1. Start by asking three fundamental questions:

    What – "What" gives you definite answers to understand the activities that are taking place or that have happened.

    How – "How" will give you the method and the flow of how the activities are happening, have already happened or shall happen.

    Why – "Why" shall give you the stories (reasoning) behind what is happening, what has happened or shall happen.

    Asking these questions in a non-threatening way will help people feel and think in the direction of the desired vision.

2. Be quiet and listen when the other person is speaking. Don't interrupt his thought process. However, do let him know through your gestures that you are paying attention.

The rule is, **One question – Two minutes of listening.**

With a few more questions, you will be able to understand the intent of the person. This will also help him perceive that you have heard him and have understood what he is trying to say.

The most important result of this is that your subordinates, or for that matter, anyone that you interact with, will perceive you as a person who can listen. Today, people have no time to listen. It is said that listening is the greatest gift you can give anyone. Your leadership will be immensely strengthened by your listening skills.

Make listening to your people your topmost priority. Realize that if you are able to listen to people, you will be able to explore more and be aware of more things. Exposure and awareness initiate change. The two together will amplify your decision-making ability.

Repetition: As a coach and influencer to various organizations, I have been able to observe one crucial element of any conversation. When someone is trying to make a point, he tries to repeat the information as well as particular actions in various forms. We, as leaders, need to develop the ability to understand the pattern in that repeated information or those actions. The day you are able to do that consciously as a leader, you will be able to understand the motives and processes of how people operate, perform, get motivated and deliver results. This stands true professionally or personally.

Note: The key to your success when it comes to people and resolving conflicts with them is your ability to understand the verbal and non-verbal clues that people give you before the conflict actually happens and taking actions proactively to avoid the conflict and mitigate the risk of non-performance and business losses.

Language: Successful leaders have the ability to comprehensively listen to the entire conversation and going by the language used, the tone and the emphasis on the words, they understand what part of the conversation they need to focus on. In this way, they can immediately link to the intent and repetition when the other person is speaking. This is physiological in nature. You and I pick up language from the kind of environment that we grow up in. If you grow up in a family where everyone is soft-spoken, respectful or calm, you will observe that your normal conversation with people goes in the same way. However, if you are brought up in an environment where everyone is bold, loud and direct, you will observe that you will speak to people the same way in your normal conversations.

Hence, it is crucial for you as a leader to understand the language that is spoken when someone is interacting with you. It gives you a lot of information about the individual – his beliefs, values, way of living and more importantly, his method of decision-making in his personal and professional life.

I have mentioned earlier that the environments/marketplaces we operate in are dynamic in nature, and so is language. This means you can hear different words from the same person in different situations, which mean the same thing. Hence, his repetition needs to be observed in context to the intention.

Observing holistically, the method of freeing yourself from the trap of labeling people is to understand the intent, repetition and language of the message when people have a conversation with you. If you *understand their intent, language and repetition*, you will also know how to create an impact *when you speak or communicate with people*. The same method can be utilized when you communicate, in the following manner:

- First, explicitly explain your intent.
- Second, select your language.
- Third, keep repeating your intent in the language that your people are comfortable with.

> **Losing Sight of Objectivity**

Let me help you understand this with a story.

This tale has a king, a queen and a prince. Theirs was a happy kingdom. Everything in and around the kingdom was flourishing as the prince was growing and his ability to lead was improving. The queen told the prince that the purpose of his life was to rule his people and ensure that he remained king until he lived. The king focused on a different teaching. He taught the prince that his purpose was to serve his people all his life, protect them and be with them through thick and thin. The young prince often used to get confused with the two different learnings that he received from his parents. One said, his duty was to serve while the other said his duty was to rule. The young prince had a first cousin whose father had passed away in a war. He was learning the same thing from both his guardians, the king and the queen. As they grew up together, the prince and his cousin were now the strong warriors of the kingdom. The prince was an obedient child, very close to his mother, and was as strong as the king.

As time passed, the prince turned to be an authoritarian, stubborn and autocratic ruler for whom everything and everybody only existed because of him. The cousin also grew to be strong but he was also humble, caring and helpful to everyone. I am sure you have heard such stories of bad kings and good kings. Naturally, none of these princes was good or bad. Everything that they did was because of the way they looked at the objectives that they intended to achieve through their actions. The truth is that whether we know it or not, all of us have a choice. Whether you exercise a choice or not, you still make a choice.

Dr. Marshall Goldsmith, the world's topmost executive coach says, "Life is easy to speak but tough to live." The tough part is making a choice that will make or break you as a leader.

Let me elaborate on what I mean by making a choice. I will explain this with examples of two exemplary leaders – Mahatma Gandhi, one of the most forgiving, non-violent leaders the world has ever witnessed and Adolf Hitler, one of the most influential dictators the world has ever seen.

Both these leaders had greater causes in their lives, which they were very passionate about. The word "passion" is a beautiful combination of two emotions, which are love and dissatisfaction with the current situation. If the desired result is not achieved, this emotion can result into dissatisfaction. This dissatisfaction, if directed well, in a more productive manner, can make miracles for the leaders and their organizations. Both these leaders loved their countries and were deeply hurt about what happened to them. However, they made a choice in their respective lives. One chose to direct his dissatisfaction through non-violence, and the other chose violence. This example will help you understand that you too, as a leader, may tremendously love something and may feel anger, frustration or stress that the result didn't turn out the way you wanted it to. Where you choose to direct the power of your dissatisfaction will decide where you as a leader take your people, your organization and your own career. You can choose to direct your anger to tackle core issues rather than directing your anger at people around you. The choice you make determines your ability as a leader. In order to make this choice in the right spirit, it is important to keep your objective in mind. Only when your objective is clear can you make the right choice.

Great leaders go through tremendous pain in the process of achieving objectivity. However, they never lose sight of objectivity and hence, dealing with pain positively creates a character that the world is in awe of. If your anger is directed in the direction of prosperity and the higher good of all, it will lead to the growth of your organization and society, and you would have made it towards being a part of the league of great leaders.

➤ **Allowing Rigidity in Processes**

The world is moving towards Volatility, Uncertainty, Complexity and Ambiguity in almost everything that we do. The famous word, "VUCA," is the acronym for these conditions.

Organizations have created processes to generate efficiency and predict the impact that they may create at the marketplace. However, if leaders create rigid processes to create impact at a marketplace which is VUCA in nature, they are setting up themselves and their organizations for failure.

When organizations grow in size horizontally or vertically, leaders need to create standardization. Although this is great and helps everyone to come on to a common platform and understanding, too much standardization also causes damage like lack of innovation, creativity, and a continuous learning culture in the company. Business decisions play an important role in making an impact on the industry you operate in. Unfortunately, the fast-moving business requirement – consumer needs – does not give the business enough time to adjust to the market's needs. Hence, most employees find it difficult to adjust to processes that are too old or constantly changing. Have you heard your employees or staff saying, "This is how it happens here," or "That's how it happens in our industry"?

People who use these words have psychologically accepted those processes as the need of their business and have reservations about change. Thus, they will show high reluctance to change. Great leaders visualize these changes, which are internal challenges in the organization. I call this, "The Challenge of NO." This is where every new idea or process is seen as a potential threat to the current systems. The typical behavior among employees or leaders in such an organization is a delay in decision-making, procrastination, going around the same thing and most importantly, distrust.

I have personally interacted with a number of leaders who are amazing when it comes to the driving process. However, the same leaders were observed to become very rigid in behavior as they had reached that greatness with a lot of discomfort that created success. They did not create agility in the process, which led the processes to be "people-averse." Because they have achieved success through some processes, they believe them to be the correct way of doing things. However, this means that if they have failed, then that process is not the correct way of doing things. Here, they don't take into account that there may be a problem with their execution and not the process. Such leaders or people don't last in a dynamic situation. Today, leaders need to be agile in the way they execute the processes leading to their organization's goals.

When I write this, I intend to make it clear that I am not saying, "Change the goal." I am saying create *guidelines* and not *rules* in order to achieve success in the process. This mechanism will help people *use their skills in order to make processes more effective*. When you have more rules and fewer guidelines in an organization, people tend to work in silos, leaders do not use their creativity and get completely occupied and content with just following the process. I term this as "the slow death of the company, or the leader in the company." The ill-effects of this are apparent when companies want to change direction or take up new goals as per the vision they have created. Hence, more effort must go into *helping people accept change rather than driving them to results.* Great leaders understand this need. Hence, when they speak to their executives about creating processes, they focus on creating guidelines and not rules. In the process, they value the creativity and innovation in their people. They will feel ownership about the work they are executing, and the process they are operating in.

> **An Environment of Fear**

The last point in the **Circle of Imbalanced Leadership** is the result of all the above four behaviors that the leader exhibits. As a result of the above four behaviors, he creates "an environment of fear." There are some signals that leaders can use to identify when they have knowingly or unknowingly created an environment of fear.

Signal 1: People's lack of commitment to work

Signal 2: Every action and thought has to be pushed through

Signal 3: People do not take ownership for their actions

Signal 4: Interdepartmental conflict

Signal 5: New ideas are unwelcome

Signal 1: People's lack of commitment to work

In an environment of fear, you will notice that people don't commit to dates, time or actions and they reply saying, "I may be able to deliver" or they do not ask questions to clarify. Such subordinates are scared about what would happen if they fail or are not able to deliver. Hence, such a response comes when they do not want to take ownership.

These are people who are disengaged in the company. Hence, we need to create an engagement strategy that excites and involves the entire workforce. The more excited and involved your workforce is, the more will be the commitment to work. This is also a phase where learning and education should be encouraged on a regular basis as part of the company's culture.

Signal 2: Every action and thought has to be pushed through

You as a leader will have difficulty in creating a system. This is the toughest time in your professional life. This happens when there are clear trust issues in the team. People are so inclined to the old ways of doing things that they do not even think of moving in a new direction. Great leaders tackle this issue by identifying the positive influencers in the team and driving the desired change through them. They are constantly communicating with the positive influencers to keep them motivated about higher causes. With strong conviction and persistence in behavior, a leader can make this change happen in people.

Signal 3: People do not take ownership for their actions

At this stage, subordinates do not take ownership for their actions, important tasks are not completed, and this creates a blame game where either the systems or people are blamed. They easily step ahead to claim recognition for everything that is a success. However, they will seldom give that credit to anyone else. This behavior is observed when people tend to prove their place in an organization, team, or group. This is a signal to the leader that an environment of fear has been created. Mistrust between employees, lack of effort, non-productive meetings, arguments rather than objective conflict, and financial results not being sound are a few direct and indirect symptoms of an environment of fear.

Let us understand this through an example. Suppose you and your team are camping in a jungle. It is a 5 nights, 6 days' camp, and you, along with four of your team members, are going for that camp. Consider that your team members don't trust each other. Will they sleep peacefully when one of the team members becomes a night watchman? It is not possible, no matter which member becomes the night watchman, because there is no trust among them. Hence, in an organization, you as a leader need to create trust within your people about each other and most importantly, about the organization. Only then will they perform better in the competitive environment, because they will feel safe working with the people and the organization they trust.

Security is the basic need of any individual, and if your organization has an environment of fear, people will not be sure of what will happen to them the next day when they go to work. Hence, focus on creating an environment that makes your employees feel safe.

Signal 4: Interdepartmental conflict

Interdepartmental conflicts are a clear sign that the top leaders of these departments do not get along. Since the leaders themselves are not aligned to the bigger cause, neither are their subordinates. That is the core reason why cross-functional teams fail. Since their leaders don't get along with each other, they too are not aligned to the cause. Great leaders solve this challenge with a formula:

Reassign → Redesign → Retrain → Replace

This 4R formula helps great leaders to get the various departments get along. In the process of **reassigning**, they shuffle leaders who do not have a contribution to make to the ongoing projects. During the **redesign stage,** they focus on reshaping the key performance areas, procedures, policies, and rules so that they are aligned to the vision, purpose, and financial goals of the organization. If that doesn't work, they **retrain** those leaders with specialized help from experts for a certain duration of time. If that doesn't work either, they are left with the last option which is to **replace.** During this process, they choose a new leader who is aligned to the company's vision, mission, and goals, who shares the same value system, and is ready to get things done objectively.

Signal 5: New ideas are unwelcome

This is a clear sign that the organization or its leaders have gotten into a clear zone of comfort and are not able to visualize the change that is required for the organization to move forward in the future. They are not able to realize that they will not exist if they do not take action. Great leaders induce and draw a picture of a change approach versus a no-change approach, and calmly let people compare it cognitively. This approach makes people realize the losses of not changing or not accepting new ideas. Great leaders are extremely optimistic and consistently find occasions to share new ideas and opportunities. They are cognitive about how the theory of Diffusion of Innovation operates and focus on the first 16 percent people who can get influenced. (This theory was developed by E. M. Rogers in 1962. Also read the book *Jumping the S-Curve*. This model is aligned to how the market reacts but can be applied to organizational change as well.) While doing this, they rely on being persistent, continuously improving themselves and transparently and openly taking feedback.

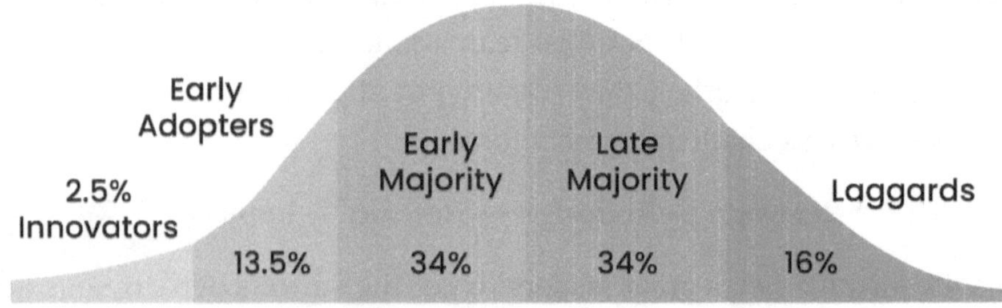

Fig. 17 Diffusion of Innovation Theory[3]

To conclude, there are certain actions that leaders must take to balance their leadership. If leaders are able to balance themselves in spite of various perceptions, biases, market volatility, complex structures, an ambiguous future, and uncertain processes, they will join the league

---

3   Diagram Reference: LaMorte, W. W. (2022, November 3). *Diffusion of innovation theory.* BUMC. https://sphweb.bumc.bu.edu/otlt/MPH-Modules/SB/BehavioralChangeTheories/BehavioralChangeTheories4.html

of great leaders. The following are the actions that leaders can take to achieve this:

➢ Take 360⁰ feedback on how your people perceive you as a leader.
➢ When you receive feedback, accept it unconditionally.
➢ Act on each step consciously with the help of an expert or coach who will stand by you during your personal journey of change.
➢ Follow all the aspects written about the change in this book.

To Summarize:

> ➢ The Circle of Imbalanced Leadership is a series of behaviors in which the leader may get trapped at any stage of his career. The five behaviors that a leader should stay away from are:

1. **Carrying past baggage** – The solution to overcome this phase is for leaders to openly accept their areas of improvement.

2. **Labeling people** – The solution for not getting into the trap of labeling people is that in any conversation, understand the three factors:

    i. Intent
    ii. Repetition and
    iii. Language

3. **Losing sight of objectivity** – Great leaders go through tremendous pain in the process of achieving objectivity. However, they never lose sight of objectivity and hence, dealing with pain positively creates a character that the world is in awe of.

4. **Allowing rigidity in processes** – When great leaders speak to their executives about creating processes, they focus on creating guidelines and not rules. In the process, they value the creativity and innovation in their people.

5. **Creating an environment of fear** – There are some signals that leaders can use to identify when they have knowingly or unknowingly created an environment of fear.

    Signal 1: People's lack of commitment to work

    Signal 2: Every action and thought has to be pushed through

    Signal 3: People do not take ownership for their actions

    Signal 4: Interdepartmental conflict

    Signal 5: New ideas are unwelcome

➢ Leaders must take certain actions, such as taking 360^0 feedback, accepting it unconditionally, and taking the help of an expert in order to balance their leadership and join the league of great leaders.

NOTES:

Your interpretation of this chapter:

Learnings that you will implement:

CHAPTER 7

HABITS OF GREAT LEADERS

"PEARL" IN THE HEART OF GREAT LEADERS

Proactivity, **E**ngagement, **A**ppreciation, **R**ecognition, and **L**istening

Before we begin this chapter, it is important to understand why the above behaviors become a MUST for you when you move ahead on the path of great leadership to create a legacy for yourself and the organization. This can be effectively explained and understood from McClelland's Theory of Needs or the Three Needs Theory or the Acquired Needs Theory, proposed by the psychologist David McClelland. This is a motivational model that explains how the three needs of Achievement, Power, and Affiliation affect the actions of people from the managerial, leadership and entrepreneurial standpoint.

Henry Murray first identified the effect of the environment on Achievement, Power and Affiliation. McClelland based his theory on Murray's list of motives and manifest needs. McClelland's Need Theory is closely associated with the Learning Theory. According to him, needs are learned or acquired by the events that people experience in their environment and culture. The **Acquired Needs Theory** was developed by David McClelland and he classified it into the Need for Achievement, Need for Power, and the Need for Affiliation and defined it as below.

Theory	Definition
Acquired Needs Theory	An individual's needs change over a period of time due to various individual experiences.
The Need for Achievement	Attainment of excellence that satisfies individual needs – internal and external.
The Need for Power	Attainment of power that satisfies the individual's need of control and security – internally and externally.
The Need for Affiliation	Attainment of social proofs by being involved and feeling a sense of belonging to various social groups.

It is important for leaders to realize that people have specific needs, and the leaders' ability to customize their behaviors according to the people is the art of Leadership Agility. This is a "must" in today's fast-moving world where people have options to move on to and are influenced by anyone around them for any reason.

As we move forward, we shall learn a little more about the Needs Theory and its relevance to today's world, how this theory can be implemented in our day-to-day life while we take business decisions based on statistics, and the advice that our people give us. We need to understand why our ability as leaders, to customize our own behavior according to existing situations, is a must.

A person's motivation, influence and effectiveness in a certain job are solely dependent on these needs of **achievement, affiliation and power** that the individual is able to source from the given organizational goals. Given below are the understandings of achievement, affiliation and power in the context of organizational performance.

Achievement: People having a high need for achievement seek to excel, and thus, tend to avoid both low-risk and high-risk situations. Achievers avoid low-risk situations as they can easily achieve success and hence, do not get the feeling of genuine achievement. In high-risk projects, achievers see the outcome as one of the chances rather than the result of putting in one's own efforts. High-achieving individuals prefer tasks that have a moderate probability of success, ideally, a fifty percent chance. Achievers also need regular feedback in order to monitor the progress of their achievements. They prefer either to work alone or with other high-achievers.

In this chapter, we explore influential behaviors that are displayed by great leaders during their interactions or conversations with various groups and teams. *You, the leader, will also realize that the key secrets to peak performance, motivation, and engagement are the need for affiliation, need for achievement and the need for power.* By applying the PEARL behaviors, you will be able to foster and trigger your teams at a deeper level that would drive your people naturally toward the purpose.

Affiliation: Those with a high need for affiliation need harmonious relationships with other people and need to feel accepted by them. They tend to conform to the norms of their work group. High-affiliation individuals prefer work that provides them with significant personal attention. They perform well when the leader gives his personal attention to their actions.

Power: A person's need for power can be of two types – personal and institutional. The person who needs institutional power (also known as social power) wants to organize efforts and people to further the goals of the organization. Entrepreneurs, leaders and managers with a high need for institutional power tend to be more effective than those with a high need for personal power. The need for personal power comes from a need for high significance and the need for institutional power comes from the need for high contribution.

PEARL in the Heart of Great Leaders

PEARL is not only an approach but also an attitude that great leaders carry throughout their performing and non-performing life. Serving people with a purpose has been the common denominator of leaders who have crafted their success stories as social leaders, business leaders, or industrialists. They have all displayed PEARL behaviors in their journey of success and failure.

I have composed the concept of the PEARL Mindset of effective leaders through my observations of great leaders and my consulting experience.

This has benefited me personally, and more importantly, it has benefited the people whom I have worked with. As leaders, all of you may be at various levels of performance when it comes to working with individuals, groups, departments or organizations. It is virtually impossible to keep mapping individuals or the groups that you lead. Hence, an approach like PEARL gives you the set of behaviors that you can use and influence individuals and groups to perform at their best with a valid cause.

1. **Proactivity: The Ability to Be Aware of Your Environment and Act**

Great leaders are aware of what is happening around them and have the courage and ability to take action. Why is proactivity a must to influence individuals and groups? Being courageous and taking action are the only skills that differentiate a great leader from every other leader. Ideas, innovations and great strategies are in vain if you do not have the courage to act proactively. The question is, where does the courage to be proactive come from?

Courage = Awareness + Ability + Faith

Great leaders enhance their awareness of their environments, understand what needs to be done, and accordingly, increase their abilities. When they do so, their faith in their abilities to solve problems increases. When a combination of all these factors comes together, it gives birth to courage. A leader who acts courageously will be perceived as proactive as he is consistently attempting to solve problems in the marketplace and in the process, creating an organization that is future-ready. He drives his organization as a torch-bearer of the newer paths that the organization wants to tread. Proactive leaders are also great change leaders. They focus on innovation and creation, with a constant urge to make the world, country, state, company, and department a better place to live and perform.

If you are in the Future, your teams remain in the Present.
If you are in the Present, your teams remain in the Past.

— Yogesh Pawar

Exercise:

Solve the questions given below. They will help you identify self-improvement areas that lie within the parameters of Awareness, Ability and Faith, which also means that you will be able to identify the gaps in knowledge, skills or attitude respectively.

1. What are the aspects of your business or work that you *lack awareness* about?

(For example: Your value system, your core beliefs, clarity about the path on which you wish to take your business operations, your ability to communicate in an influential manner, your human resource mechanism, your operational mechanism, and your financial mechanism.)

____

____

____

____

____

2. What are the aspects of your business or work that you *lack ability* in?

____

____

____

____

____

3. What are the aspects of your business or work that you *lack faith* in?

____

____

____

____

____

Remember, you live in five different environments – personal, professional, social, family and spiritual. It is the same for the people around you. Hence, everyone around you will either have less or more awareness, less or more ability, and less or more faith in something that you wish them to act on proactively. Therefore, it is your moral duty to get them on to the same path of awareness, ability and faith that you are on. All these actions that you take keeping in mind the organization's vision will help you move faster with accuracy in your decisions. These decisions will lead you to bring out a great leader who is hidden inside you. **Once you are able to master the three attributes of Awareness, Ability and Faith, your decision-making will be faster, which people will perceive as Proactivity.**

Most importantly, you will be a leader with courage. When you perform acts that are perceived as impossible, people call you courageous. However, everyone who has taken courageous actions in their personal or professional lives has had clarity about what they wanted, where they wanted to go and why. Your awareness, ability and faith toward a goal will help you perform faster; this will lead to your proactiveness.

You may fail in those proactive actions too. They may be taken too early or may lack precision. However, every time you take a proactive step, one result is certain – you will learn "how to do it or how not to do it."

Most of us, in due course of time, become less proactive and even reactive due to lack of awareness, lack of ability to execute, and lack of faith. The result is that we lose the courage to take action, procrastinate, and also lose time.

> *Proactivity is a courageous action taken by people who have awareness, ability and faith.*
>
> – *Yogesh Pawar*

Exercise:

In the table below, rate yourself from 1 to 10. This self-evaluation will make you aware of your state of proactivity in life or business. You will be able to identify the aspects you wish to improve. And if you focus and act on them, it will show a noticeable change in you as a human being.It will also positively affect your leadership because it instills awareness in you as a leader, which leads to a trigger to learn and make yourself able. I personally do this every year and find that my priorities keep changing. Thus, my proactive actions change too. There is no need to defend yourself and blame others. Rather, what is required is to increase one's patience to work on these aspects and be more courageous while taking action for things that are really meaningful for one as a leader.

Learning	
Health	
Spouse, Kids	
Parents	
Customers	
Employees, Subordinates or Supervisors	
Friends	
Financials	
Experience Sharing	
Adoption of Technology	

Fig. 18 Your state of Proactivity in Life/Business

How proactive are you?

I am sure you have realized that there are many aspects of your life and business that you can be proactive in and make a change that can lead you toward your vision. Great leaders not only focus on themselves, but also wire themselves to assist others in their journey. Thus, be aware, be able and have faith that you can assist people around you. Psychologically, you are assisting them to feel capable, secure, and create social proof. This will keep them motivated for the bigger cause that you have for them.

As a result, what you will get is the "Reciprocation Effect." People around you will start copying your behavior. Ask your immediate subordinates the following questions:

1. What are their top three professional goals and how you can support them?

____

____

____

2. What are the top three learnings that they would need support from you on?

____

____

____

3. What are the top three things that you can help them with immediately at their workplace?

____

____

____

When you get the answers to these three questions, be honest to yourself about what you can do for them and act on it. Give it a place on your agenda and see the magic happening in 90 days. There are great chances that your subordinates or anyone around you that you are consciously focusing on to improve, will start reciprocating to your proactivity and will replicate your behaviors. Thereafter, repeat this activity every month.

Between stimulus and response, there is a space. In that space is our power to choose our response. In our response, lies our growth and freedom.

– Viktor E. Frankl
*(Author of **Man's Search for Meaning**)*

2. Engagement: The Ability to Get Along With People

Why is engagement a "must" behavior in today's leadership?

"According to our recent *State of the Global Workplace* report, 85% of employees are not engaged or are actively disengaged at work. The economic consequences of this global 'norm' are approximately $7 trillion in lost productivity. Eighteen percent are actively disengaged in their work and workplace, while 67% are 'not engaged.'"[4]

Why is the number of employees disengaged so high? This is purely because the leaders who work with them are not able to create a common cause for them to perform. There is another side to the story too. Organizations attempt to give the best packages, best perks and best facilities but forget to create the best *cause* for the employees to put in their blood, sweat and tears and make them work for paychecks and perks instead.

Simon Sinek mentions and elaborates this aspect of a leader's behavior with amazing clarity. (Strong recommendation for reference reading: *Start with Why: How Great Leaders Inspire Everyone to Take Action*) Your people can only be engaged with a cause; a cause that is bigger than the paycheck and which gives them the motive to wake up early and sleep a little late. The elements of a bigger cause – a purpose, a reason for them to perform every day with the same rigor and passion needs to be crafted by the leader based on the vision, mission, and value system of the organization. Most leaders fall short in creating an emotional engagement with people. All large organizations today were small in the past. They were able to grow because their people had a never-say-die spirit and were strongly connected with a cause. It is the leader's responsibility to create more leaders like himself who run for a cause. The failure of the leader to create an affiliation with a bigger cause will

---

4   Harter, J. Dismal employee engagement is a sign of global mismanagement. *Gallup.*   https://www.gallup.com/workplace/231668/dismal-employee-engagement-sign-global-mismanagement.aspx

make people at the mid or bottom of the organization pyramid feel left out. Thus, constant communication or connect until the last level is the most important ability that great leaders possess. By doing this, you will be able to create more leaders in the organization and bind people together with a common thought process.

The issue is how you, as a leader, can achieve that. Not only must your words or your speeches be engaging (that is the minimum threshold required now), but you must also have the ability to stand at the gates of your company, put your hand on the shoulder of an employee and ask, "How's it going?", "How do you feel about working here?" This ability will lead to a positive wave in the organization that will spread like wildfire. People love to be noticed and if you start noticing them, they remember you, and that is the key to keep them engaged. Just like employee performance is important, so is your ability to maintain and enhance your relationship with each employee no matter what level he is at in the organization. Find innovative methods to engage with different people in the various departments of your organization.

A few points to remember:

- Make it your daily habit to engage with your people.
- Also, do engage with people who don't report to you.
- Engage with people who are at the lower levels in the value chain.
- When you go to meet your customers, engage with their other departments.
- When you go to restaurants, engage with the owner.
- When you go to exhibitions, engage with your competition.
- This is not networking; this is pure interaction to make friends. (Make it a point to put a smile on the other person's face – THAT'S YOUR JOB.)

> *Leadership is hard to define, and good leadership, even harder. But if you can get people to follow you to the ends of the earth, you are a great leader.*
>
> *– Indra Nooyi*

Exercise:

In the table below, rate yourself on a scale of 1 to 10 to identify your levels of engagement with various people.

Family	
Subordinates	
Superiors	
Support Functions	
Friends	
Bankers/Investors	
Social Acquaintances	
Self- Education	
Hobbies	
Spiritual Activities	

Fig. 19 Your levels of Engagement with Various People

As humans, we are social animals and always find ways to be with communities that support our values and belief systems. This could be through places of worship, associations, collaborations, NGOs or social organizations. People with common beliefs and value systems can be found together. People come to such places by choice and do what they can for others. The same is with the organization. Hence, you need to create a common value system in the company and ensure that your employee engagement plans revolve around it. Every action should match your organization's value system. This is the only way to induce a belief in people (As mentioned in Chapter 1, repetition of information in various forms, over a period of time creates a belief system).

In reference to your value systems, what five actions will you take to engage your employees in two ways (One-to-Group and One-to-One)?

How will you as a leader ENGAGE externally and internally with all the stakeholders impacting the organization and your professional life? Refer to the chart and do this exercise by following the example of the value of Ownership given below.

Organizational Value	Value Definition	Top 5 Actions for Engagement
I. Ownership	Taking measures proactively wherever required	1. Organization leaders meeting top 50 customers every quarter
		2. Building products and services innovatively before the competition
		3. Interacting with the top leaders personally at regular intervals to build relationships
		4. Having proactive conversations with bankers and investors
		5. Contribution and sharing for sector upgradation

Organizational Value	Value Definition	Top 5 Actions for Engagement
II.		1.
		2.
		3.
		4.
		5.

Organizational Value	Value Definition	Top 5 Actions for Engagement
III.		1.
		2.
		3.
		4.
		5.

Organizational Value	Value Definition	Top 5 Actions for Engagement
IV.		1.
		2.
		3.
		4.
		5.

Organizational Value	Value Definition	Top 5 Actions for Engagement
V.		1.
		2.
		3.
		4.
		5.

Organizational Value	Value Definition	Top 5 Actions for Engagement
VI.		1.
		2.
		3.
		4.
		5.

3. Appreciate: The Ability to Find Good in Others

Our body has a virtual radar that works 24x7 and throws back all the information that we have stored in our memory. This virtual radar is called the Reticular Activating System of our body (RAS). RAS is very powerful, and it throws back all your experiences to you when you meet a similar experience in the present situation. Let us take an example. When you want to buy a house, you suddenly start noticing such advertisements in the newspaper or on your television or on billboards. Have you ever thought why this happens? This is your RAS working. Similarly, when you buy a new car of a specific make, you start noticing the same make or model faster than anyone around you who doesn't own the same make or model. RAS functions to give you information before you make a decision, and helps you justify your decision after you have made it.

The mechanisms of our body and mind are defined by the kind of memories we store in our brain. Although it is not humanly possible to have only good experiences every day, it is absolutely possible to decide which experience to choose and preserve and for how long in your memory.

> *You become what you think, you think what you feel and you feel what you experience. So, be mindful.*
>
> *– Yogesh Pawar*

Choosing which memory to preserve is a choice a leader has. This choice will define his destiny. Leaders must develop the ability to consciously make choices that will help them have a clutter-free mind – a mind that is focused on the objectives and the bigger vision that they are creating for themselves and the organization they work for. It is absolutely possible to choose the experiences that you want to relate to or give the other person around you.

Approximately 60% of subordinates or family members who are disengaged have one big issue with leaders or other family members – they don't feel appreciated. Remember, all behaviors that are appreciated, either positively or negatively, tend to be repeated. Hence, leaders choose to observe positive behaviors and appreciate people around them consciously. Remember that all those behaviors with your subordinates, leaders, colleagues, friends, parents, spouse, and kids will be repeated if they are appreciated.

An important question is "Do you like to be appreciated?" I am sure the answer is a firm "Yes!" However, "WHAT" should be appreciated becomes a big challenge with leaders due to the various dynamics involved including the leader's personality, his definition of excellence, his definition of great or good work, and his expectations from people around him. There are also some global taboos attached to appreciation like:

"Too much of appreciation is not good."

"If I appreciate people every time, they will take me for granted as a leader."

"If I tell them what I appreciate, they will only perform those tasks."

This one is classy. "Never appreciate your spouse in front of your in-laws." (This is generally prevalent in the Asian continent.)

All of the above global taboos or assumptions disregard the basic need for social affiliation and recognition. It is our inability to understand

and choose what to appreciate that leads to these assumptions. Let us understand this through a case study.

Case Study

This is the story of a CEO of a manufacturing company in Delhi, India, who I have been coaching for over six months now. Through him, we built the value system of his organization, defined a new vision, a new mission and helped him make a plan for the company to grow ten times in the next three years. During one of the coaching sessions, he narrated a challenge he was facing with an employee.

The employee, a supervisor at the plant level, had been working efficiently for the last ten years, since the inception of the business. He was also among the first few to join the company during its startup days. The company has now grown to employ over 500 people, and for the last ten years, this person was working as a floor supervisor, manning the production floor and blue-collar employees. During his initial years, he was directly connected to the CEO due to the small size of the team. However, as the team grew, there were shift managers, plant managers and a plant head above him. His access to the CEO was now minimal. However, he personally made it a point to report the daily production to the CEO directly. On the other hand, the CEO was also comfortable getting the data from him for clarity and comparison.

During one of the working days, it was reported to the CEO that the supervisor had misbehaved and spoken rudely to the employees, due to which, three of the employees had resigned. The CEO called the supervisor to his cabin and helped him understand that this would not be tolerated and that he shouldn't repeat his mistake. With complete sincerity, the supervisor assured the CEO that this would not happen again. The issue was closed for the moment. However, a month later, the same thing happened. The supervisor once again promised that he wouldn't repeat such behavior. However, such incidents kept happening almost every month.

As per the usual HR practices, a letter warning the employee needs to be issued, following which, if the behavior continues, the employee must be terminated on the grounds of misconduct. A developmental approach says that he should be coached since he is an efficient employee and has been an asset for a decade.

People in the company felt that he was taking advantage of being in the CEO's good books. The CEO knew that although he was rude, he was good at his work and at following the timelines. But, all said and done, he didn't want to encourage a culture of jealousy and disharmony in the organization.

During the coaching conversation with the CEO, we decided that since there was no incident of untrustworthy or dishonest behavior, certain actions to tweak his performance could be taken:

Action 1: Call the employee and appreciate his work.

Action 2: Give least importance to the issue of bad behavior.

Action 3: Motivate him to repeat his good actions or behaviors.

Action 4: Focus on the benefits of the good behavior that he has displayed in the past.

Anything that is appreciated is repeated. Noticing bad behavior and repeatedly talking about it also creates a feeling of recognition, although negatively. Hence, repeating and harnessing the positive behaviors will always be of greater value while developing people in the organization. Also, as an individual goes through this kind of experience, he will tend to repeat a similar developmental approach in case of other people, once he gains a leadership position.

Anything that you focus on, amplifies. Anything that is amplified is executed.

— Yogesh Pawar

After around six such visits of the employee to his cabin, the CEO started getting feedback from the plant head and managers that the employee was treating his workers well. This is the magic of noticing the good in others!

Appreciate people wholeheartedly and they will repeat those behaviors. The best part about noticing good things in others is that you as a leader will get into a pattern or habit of noticing everything around you that is good. As the Law of Attraction says, "You shall get what you seek."

This process makes you a happier individual. You become more energetic as you are able to notice opportunities faster and quicker than people around you, whether in business or personal life. Finally, this makes you more humble and grateful as a human being.

Activity: Attempt the following questionnaire and observe how often you appreciate others. Rate yourself on a scale from 5 to 1.

Always: 5, Often: 4, Sometimes: 3, Seldom: 2, Never: 1

Parameters	Always	Often	Sometimes	Seldom	Never
I notice and appreciate my subordinate's work when he presents his ideas to me.					
I acknowledge every email which deserves appreciation.					
I am able to notice the errors in my subordinate's work.					

Parameters	Always	Often	Sometimes	Seldom	Never
I expect to have a detailed understanding of every job that is being done by my subordinate.					
I notice the little things kept on my subordinate's desk.					
I notice and appreciate my subordinate's dressing style.					
I notice and appreciate my subordinate's ability to lead a meeting.					
I notice and appreciate a complex challenge resolved by my subordinate.					
I give challenging tasks to my subordinates.					

Parameters	Always	Often	Sometimes	Seldom	Never
I tend to be more vocal about my expectations with all my subordinates.					

Scores: 50 to 45: You are either naturally gifted to notice good things around you, or have overrated yourself (be honest; the exercise is for self-evaluation). If you are naturally gifted, harness this power to make a greater impact on people around you and help them become great leaders under your able leadership.

Scores: 44 to 35: You are subjective in your appreciation. Most of the time, you are in a dilemma about whether something has to be appreciated or not. Make a choice. It causes no harm if you appreciate the people around you. Not only would you make yourself a better leader, but you will also develop other leaders, besides developing your own abilities.

A score below 34: A lot of good things around you are going unnoticed. If you do take notice of such things, it will add great value to your and other people's lives. Get your assumptions of negativity out of your mind and look at things objectively.

Note: There are high possibilities that you have worked with a team for a long period of time and hence, have tremendous comfort in all interactions. These teams break due to overexposure to each other.

4. **Recognition: The Ability to Announce Good Things about Others Publicly**

One of the strongest human needs is that of social affiliation. People around us need to constantly get feedback in terms of how well they do their task. It doesn't stop there. As leaders, it becomes our personal responsibility to announce all the good things that people in the organization are doing, publicly. Whether online or offline, leaders need to take personal interest in highlighting these aspects of their people's work.

Remember, leaders who recognize others' mistakes publicly are also anchoring the thought of public humiliation. Hence, my personal recommendation is that if you wish to give negative feedback, do it in person and use the learnings of the failure as cases of improvement.

We all love to be appreciated. However, one of the greatest triggers of human motivation is recognition. I will elaborate further.

Million-dollar businesses are based on this one word called "social affiliation" (recognition). If we closely observe every online social platform – Facebook, Twitter, Instagram, LinkedIn, YouTube, Google Plus, Quora or Tinder, all of these operate on two basic fundamentals:

1. They satisfy your need to be appreciated (positively or negatively)
2. They satisfy your need to be recognized (positively or negatively)

You may check any social networking site, formal or informal; it **appreciates**, or **recognizes** actions. The more the action is **appreciated**, the more it is **recognized**. The social term is called "GOING VIRAL." The definition of this phrase means that something has been appreciated or recognized by a large number of people. If you notice, similar kinds of photos, videos or articles start getting promoted all throughout the web. As people keep sharing, those posts get appreciated or are recognized and start getting circulated to a larger and larger audience.

Sharing and Recognition are used as great tools to inspire people to give their best at work. Every leader can use them in his daily work, and they drive performance in humans.

When we share and recognize the efforts of an individual or group of people, it is a declaration that the individual or group has done three things.

> ➤ It reaffirms that the act performed is right, and has benefited the organization in a certain way.
> ➤ It raises the belief in an individual or group to repeat the actions.
> ➤ It encourages the people around them to perform similar acts to experience the same feeling of recognition, which leads to leveraging performance in people.

Hence, sharing and recognition can act as stimulants to human motivation and create a multiplier effect on performance. More importantly, humans believe they all want to be a part of the elite group in the organization that is being noticed and appreciated by people all over the company. We all want to be in a community or a group that has social acceptance. All humans believe that they are unique, and everyone wants to be part of a group that gives its best performance, and creates great stories. Hence, we constantly speak about our specialities and uniqueness to everyone, whether in interviews, in projects or ideas that we execute. It is this uniqueness that we all want to represent and which keeps us going toward our real achievements and drives us towards our goals.

It is now important to understand what to appreciate or recognize. Throughout this book, we have focused on how imperative the vision, mission and values of the company are, that the leaders in the organization have created/upheld. Assuming that you are the torchbearer of the organization's vision, mission and values with honesty and integrity, and are fully committed to achieving them, your next step is to notice every action or organizational goal that supports your vision, mission or values that needs to be appreciated and recognized.

> *Your engagement, appreciation and recognition are directly proportional to the impact your people will create in the marketplace.*
>
> *– Yogesh Pawar*

The following are actions that you can take to recognize people personally.

1. **Trigger Step:** Link recognition and your appreciation to the organization's vision, mission and values.

2. **Incremental Step:** Recognize incremental steps, like people who complete tasks before the deadline, proactive actions that people take, *kaizens* and innovations in the process, or when people get along as friends in the team, or when they support each other to deliver actions that support the cause.

3. **Make it your personal habit:** Be continuously and consistently conscious about recognizing people. Let people perceive that you recognize every effort towards the organization's vision, mission, and values.

4. **Make it significant:** Give the other person fair weightage for their actions – actions that they take to move forward every day.

5. **Make it spontaneous:** Don't wait for an event to recognize people. Let it come from the heart and immediately as soon as the task is completed. We live in a world of instant gratification. Hence, it is logical to appreciate people instantly if we want them to repeat their actions.

Exercise:

Note three actions that you expect from people that are aligned to your organization's Vision.

____

____

____

Note three actions that you expect from people that are aligned to your organization's Mission.

____

____

____

Note three actions that you expect from people that are aligned to your organization's Goals.

____

____

____

Unless you identify the actions that you expect, you will not be able to recognize and appreciate them. Now that you have written them down, you are aware of what actions to recognize and appreciate.

5. Listen: The Ability to Make People Comfortable

When I first established this definition of listening i.e. to make people comfortable, I was personally satisfied with what came out of my mind. The definition brought back many important conversations that I have had professionally or personally throughout my life. I realized that during every conversation that I had had, which led to conflicts or arguments, I was not able to make the other person comfortable.

Hence, very consciously, I started practicing the art of listening, and as a result, I started making more friends professionally and personally.

If you ask yourself, "Why do I like a particular friend?", I am sure one of the important answers you may give is that because he or she listens to you and makes you comfortable.

Whether it is a relationship between husband-wife, father-son, leader-subordinate or peer-to-peer, unless the other person feels comfortable, you will never be able to inspire him to act toward the desired goal. As a professional coach and consultant, I have realized through years of practice that "listening" is the key to success.

Listening is an "art," but understanding the science behind it is very important. When you are listening, you get ample time to churn your own thoughts and assumptions that you hold about the conversation and the subject. Around 60 percent of your conversations will mostly be with people who are professional acquaintances or are personally related to you. When you begin to focus on the other person's speech completely – words, expressions, tone and emotions, your *neuro systems* get enough information to process. Due to this, the possibility of you being accurate to the context or objectives becomes far higher and it also allows you to clear your assumptions.

This makes your decision-making, analytical and strategic thinking far better. Now, let us understand the art of listening through a case study.

Case Study

Sanjeev Gupta was a Sr. Manager in an IT company in Dubai for whom we were working on a consulting assignment in 2015-16. He handled huge service delivery projects for the company with his well-trained engineers. He had a project team of around 560 people with ten direct reportees, a second line of reportees and system engineers. Viraj Mehta, his manager, was an extremely talented professional and led a team of project leads and system engineers. During the course of our work,

Viraj expressed that Sanjeev was a wonderful leader and that he liked to work under his supervision. When questioned why he felt so, he narrated the following experiences that emphasize the importance of the art of listening.

Viraj said, "Sanjeev is always open to ideas and allows me to make decisions. He guides me and gives me a pleasant feeling of achievement. But he never, or seldom, gives answers. Sometimes, this is annoying but it allows me to think and come up with my own solutions, and he only questions me for clarification. The best part is, he never or very rarely, says no. But when he must, he uses phrases like, "Please help me find clarity," or "May I advise...?" After completing the sentence, he states that the decision is entirely mine. Most of the times, the decisions I make after this conversation are more accurate and relevant to the organization's goals. After this process, he always says, "You took a good decision," and appreciates and recognizes me. Hence, I love to work with a leader who gives me my space, questions my assumptions and appreciates my decisions."

I am sure you too have observed what Sanjeev does. He

> ➢ Gives his employees the correct environment
> ➢ Questions them
> ➢ Asks them for clarity
> ➢ Appreciates or recognizes them regularly

It is a simple four-step process that makes people feel that their leader is interested in listening to them. In the end, your people want to feel that they are heard, and this makes them feel secure and happy in the journey towards achieving goals.

The art of listening is my personal favorite action that I take while leading people. It has not just made me a better professional but also a better son, father, husband and friend.

> *When you give a decision and say "no," you have to use your energy to justify it. But instead of saying no, when you ask the question "why," the other person needs to use his energy. In the process, it clears the assumptions of both parties, and leads to better mutual decisions.*
>
> *– Yogesh Pawar*

To Summarize:

> ➢ People have specific needs, and the ability of leaders to customize their behaviors according to people is the art of **Leadership Agility.**

> ➢ **The Acquired Needs Theory** was developed by David McClelland and he classified it into the **Need for Achievement, Need for Power and the Need for Affiliation.**

> ➢ **PEARL** is not only an approach but also an attitude that great leaders carry throughout their performing and non-performing life.

1. Proactivity: The ability to be aware of your environment and act
2. Engagement: The ability to get along with people
3. Appreciate: The ability to find the good in others
4. Recognition: The ability to announce good things about others publicly
5. Listen: The ability to make people comfortable

NOTES:

Your interpretation of this chapter:

Learnings that you will implement:

PEARL™

Proactivity | Engagement | Appreciation | Recognition | Listen

PEARL in the heart of great leaders is an art to be acquired and like any other art, it needs to be practiced consciously. In order to have positive experiences of the application of PEARL, below is a challenge that you may want to take up.

The 21-Day Challenge for PEARL Implementation

PEARL	Number of people you will impact	Relationship with the people you will impact	Actions you will take personally
Proactivity			
Engagement			
Appreciation			
Recognition			
Listening			

With this book, I would like to invite you to join the School of Inspirational Leadership (SIL) in the journey of learning, living and growing together. If this book has made a difference to your approach and given you a broader perspective, and you look forward to more of such learning across various fields, from people with vast experience and expertise, log on to www.siluniversity.com or scan the QR code given below.

Fig. 20 QR Code – www.siluniversity.com

You will be introduced to a huge vista of up-to-date learning through state-of-the-art technology and what's more, you can benefit from one-to-one as well as group interactions.

With this book, our journey of seeking an important quality of the business world – Effective Leadership – has just begun.

The Learning Culture at SIL

With the next generation fast embracing entrepreneurship, there is a need for practical business learning and guidance on sustaining and growing businesses. The School of Inspirational Leadership (SIL) is India's first Edutainment and Consulting organization that provides learning programs, consulting and advisory services to startups, SME, MSME, and ME entrepreneurs, to achieve the business growth they have set their sights on.

See you in this meaningful, engaging and enjoyable journey! Let's learn, evolve and grow together. Cheers!

ABOUT THE AUTHOR

An entrepreneur, author and speaker, Yogesh comes with a fantastic understanding of business and people. With a Ph.D. in Predictive Psychology and around two decades of professional experience, he extensively guides and coaches leaders in emerging economies in the Asian, Gulf and African regions.

Due to his positive approach and keen observation of people's behaviors, his USP as a speaker and a coach is that he can create Simplicity, Efficiency, and Impact for businesses in the marketplace. His work is filled with energy, humor, science, art, leadership and innovation.

He is the founder and managing partner of SIL (School of Inspirational Leadership), a unique institute for entrepreneurs, based in Pune, India. The school focuses on strategies that create an environment of success and scalability in business.

He is the chairman of ARISE (Association of Rising and Inspiring Syndicate of Entrepreneurs), a community of entrepreneurs coming together across India to solve common business problems through sharing and using the power of collective bargaining.

His unorthodox and unconventional ways of expressing his ideas have earned him quite a name. Both shy and energetic at the same time, these contrasting qualities make him stand out all the more, and pleasantly surprise his audiences.

BIBLIOGRAPHY

1. The Conscious Competence Learning Model – Neol Burch
2. Emotional Drivers of Performance – Arthur F. Carmazzi
3. Theory of Motivation – David McClelland
4. Blue Ocean Strategy: How to Create Uncontested Market Space and Make the Competition Irrelevant, W. Chan Kim and Renée Mauborgne
5. Jack Welch and The 4E's of Leadership: How to Put GE's Leadership Formula to Work in Your Organization, Jeffrey A. Krames
6. Nitishastra – Chanakya